ASKING
about Asking

Mastering the Art of Conversational Fundraising

M. Kent Stroman, CFRE

ASKING

about Asking

Mastering the Art of Conversational Fundraising

PROPERTY OF

MAY 1 3 2011

THE FOUNDATION CTR

*Charity*Channel

PRESS
™

Asking about Asking: Mastering the Art of Conversational Fundraising™
One of the **In the Trenches**™ series
Published by
CharityChannel Press, an imprint of CharityChannel LLC
30021 Tomas, Suite 300
Rancho Santa Margarita, CA 92688-2128 USA

www.charitychannel.com

Copyright © 2011 by M. Kent Stroman
"Conversational Fundraising" is a trademark of M. Kent Stroman.

All rights reserved. No part of this book shall be reproduced, stored in a retrieval system, or transmitted by any means, electronic, mechanical, photocopying, recording, or otherwise, without written permission from the publisher. No patent liability is assumed with respect to the use of the information contained herein. This publication contains the opinions and ideas of its author. It is intended to provide helpful and informative material on the subject matter covered. It is sold with the understanding that the author and publisher are not engaged in rendering professional services in the book. If the reader requires personal assistance or advice, a competent professional should be consulted. The author and publisher specifically disclaim any responsibility for any liability, loss, or risk, personal or otherwise, which is incurred as a consequence, directly or indirectly, of the use and application of any of the contents of this book. Although every precaution has been taken in the preparation of this book, the publisher and author assume no responsibility for errors or omissions. No liability is assumed for damages resulting from the use of information contained herein. The characters portrayed in this book's "Cast of Characters," and the events associated with them, are fictitious. Any similarity to real persons, living or dead, is coincidental and not intended.

In the Trenches, In the Trenches logo, and book design are trademarks of CharityChannel Press, an imprint of CharityChannel LLC.

ISBN: 978-0-9841580-3-4
Library of Congress Control Number: 2011923270

13 12 11 10 8 7 6 5 4 3 2 1

Printed in the United States of America

This and most CharityChannel Press books are available at special quantity discounts for bulk purchases for sales promotions, premiums, fundraising, or educational use. For information, contact CharityChannel Press, 30021 Tomas, Suite 300, Rancho Santa Margarita, CA 92688-2128 USA. +1 949-589-5938

About the Author

M. Kent Stroman

Kent is President of Stroman & Associates, providing consulting services for nonprofit organizations in capital campaigns, board governance, strategic planning and leadership development.

Kent's purpose in life is to *equip, inspire and encourage.* He accomplishes this through speaking, writing, teaching and consulting.

For decades he has been engaged in business and organizational leadership; helping numerous organizations achieve their goals, fulfill their dreams and maximize their potential with his passion for excellence. Kent is a Certified Fund Raising Executive (CFRE) and has been personally involved in generating tens of millions of dollars for charitable causes. He has been named Outstanding Fundraising Executive by Eastern Oklahoma's Association of Fundraising Professionals (AFP).

He is a BoardSource-trained governance consultant, Sarkeys Foundation-approved retreat facilitator, and serves as an adjunct consultant for the Oklahoma Center for Nonprofits.

Kent is a graduate of the AFP Faculty Training Academy, earning the designation of Master Trainer. He has trained hundreds of professionals in various aspects of fundraising, leadership and management.

In addition to a vast portfolio of board experience, Kent regularly volunteers on behalf of numerous organizations. Kent was honored by Big Brothers Big Sisters with the cherished Ray G. Steiner "Champions" Award for "exemplifying the character qualities of leadership by example, integrity, generosity, and commitment to excellence; and for outstanding contributions to furthering the mission of Big Brothers Big Sisters."

Kent has been married to Marva for thirty-two years. Together they have three children and five grandchildren.

Kent is a frequent speaker and presenter to regional, national and international audiences.

Dedication

Just two weeks before I submitted this manuscript to my editor, Jim Pritchard passed away at the age of eighty-eight. Having named him several times in the text that follows, Jim's influence was already firmly entrenched herein. Suddenly, numerous reasons began to emerge as to why it would be absolutely perfect for *Asking about Asking* to be dedicated to the life and legacy of Jim.

I met Jim Pritchard before I joined the fundraising profession. He had recently made a very generous contribution of appreciated stock to the charitable organization for which I worked at the time.

There is no way I could have imagined the impact this one person would have on my life: professionally and personally. I didn't even realize how much Jim had influenced me until the day after his death.

The phone in my office rang and the voice at the other end of the call identified herself as a newspaper reporter. "I'd like to get your input for the front page article of today's edition," she explained. Without pausing she continued, "I understand you knew Jim Pritchard quite well and I hope you can fill in some blanks for me." She had unknowingly touched a nerve within me. Several minutes later, when the call was over, I began to tally the influence this man's life had on me. Before the call I knew it was significant. Afterwards I realized that no other person had prepared me for success in fundraising more than Dr. James Edward Pritchard.

I would love to share all the things I learned from Jim. You will read some of them in the pages that follow. But I dedicate this book to the legacy and memory of Jim because he was a:

- ◆ brilliant scientist;
- ◆ compassionate friend;
- ◆ dedicated father;
- ◆ faithful Christian;
- ◆ fearless leader;
- ◆ fierce competitor;
- ◆ generous donor;
- ◆ intelligent thinker;
- ◆ life-long learner;
- ◆ loving husband;
- ◆ persistent problem solver;
- ◆ visionary planner; and
- ◆ willing volunteer.

Jim was always on a mission—usually more than one at any given time! Yet he could always find the time and energy to help others in need. My prayer is that the influence Jim had on me will be multiplied thousands of times over as others read these pages and, just as I have done, put Jim's wisdom to practical use and advance charitable causes.

Asking about Asking is dedicated to Jim's legacy of willingly giving his own time, energy and financial resources to improve the lives of others. May all who read these pages be inspired to 'go and do likewise.'

Acknowledgements

If I were to name everyone who has contributed directly or indirectly to my writing this book it would be twice as long. I'll have to settle with naming these selfless people who have graciously added value to my life.

Were it not for a 'chance' conversation with Jim Whitt, I would never have considered one day writing a book. Thank you, Jim.

For years my colleague and friend, Kathy Wright, faithfully prompted, challenged, corrected and refined my work. Thank you, Kathy.

Without Matt Pendergraff, the most creative person I know, and designer, Natalie Turner, there would be no wonderful depiction of *The 10 Step Staircase*. Thank you, Matt and Natalie.

No one reviewed and evaluated the text more thoroughly than Brenda Meyers, my friend of thirty-four years. Thank you, Brenda.

We've all heard how ruthless an editor can be, but that has not been my experience. Linda Lysakowski encouraged, enhanced and endured the writing of this manuscript. Thank you, Linda.

Stephen Nill at CharityChannel Press patiently shepherded the entire process. Thank you, Steve.

Most important to me is Marva Stroman, my loving wife, inspiring companion and best friend in the whole world. She believes in me. Thank you, Marva.

M. Kent Stroman

Contents

Foreword

Money creates more confusion and chaos in people's lives today than almost anything else. We are bombarded constantly with messages telling us what we should do with our money. In the final analysis, there are only three things anyone can do with money: Money can be spent, saved or given away. It is important to note that to have a balanced financial plan and a balanced life you must spend, save, and give a part of every dollar. As in most areas of life, this balance is what keeps us happy and sustains us.

One needs only to look at the personal, corporate, and government deficits to understand we are doing a great job spending our money. Bookstores are jammed with volumes—including some of my own—explaining how we should save and invest our funds.

Asking About Asking deals with the elusive and hard-to-grasp topic of how effective fundraisers should approach and manage givers. When we solicit funds, we always endeavor to create a win-win situation. The beneficiary of the money has a clear and obvious benefit; however, the donor can take just as much away from the transaction even though this benefit is sometimes harder to understand and quantify. We all have the need to be givers. Stroman astutely reveals how we can help people effectively and efficiently plan and implement their donations to achieve this win-win.

I have heard it said that the most fun we can ever have with money is giving it away. I will admit as I was struggling financially through my early adult years I found such statements to be bewildering. Today, I have my own foundation as well as a dedicated college scholarship that is in its twenty-second year—having provided over five hundred scholarships to deserving young people. Through my book, *The Ultimate Gift*, and the subsequent movie based on it, I have had the opportunity to speak to many families of wealth and philanthropic organizations about planning their giving.

Helping donors to be prudent givers is as difficult as helping people to become prudent investors. As he was giving away billions of dollars Bill Gates conceded that giving money away is harder than earning it in the first place. Mr. Gates understands that it's more than just writing a check. It's understanding the needs of people around the world as well as your own need to become a giver.

Helping people to understand and manage this process is among the highest callings of human endeavor. None of us need help spending our money, and it's hard to turn around without being confronted by someone wanting to help us invest our money, but it is a rare individual, indeed, who wants to listen enough to understand our philanthropic goals and help us make those goals become a reality.

As you read these pages, I hope you will think about your own role as a giver and how you can help other organizations and individuals clarify their own giving. There has never been a time when more people need to give and receive well-placed gifts.

If you ever need the assistance of someone else in life's major endeavors, you need to explore these pages. If you desire to secure larger gifts without 'wearing out your welcome,' read on. If you wish to inspire donors to enrich their lives by giving more generously, just turn the page!

Jim Stovall
President, Narrative Television Network
Entrepreneur of the Year, 1997
International Humanitarian of the Year, 2000
Author, *The Ultimate Gift*

October 2010

Preface

Before you begin to wade your way through these pages, let me offer a few thoughts about what this book *is*—and *isn't*.

It's *not*...

...a treatise on *getting* something for one's self.

...an instruction manual for telling groups of people to "pull out your checkbook and get on board with the rest of us."

...the promotion of a 'game,' 'ploy,' 'trick' or 'clever technique' to get people to do what they really don't want to do.

...about *taking* something away from one person to help someone else (the Robin Hood syndrome).

...new ways of stating our gift *expectations* to prospects.

But *it is*...

...a guidebook on *receiving* for the sake of others (aka mission).

...about asking one donor (individual, family, business or foundation) for a specific gift at a specific time for a specific purpose.

...solid advice on ways to invite prospective donors to make an informed decision about *if, how* and *when* they might support a given charitable cause.

...a pathway to *accepting* heartfelt contributions willingly offered and meaningfully used.

...a fresh approach to sharing a message of hopeful inspiration to generous giving.

...a quick and easy one-step solution to all your fundraising events (what I call *"drive-by fundraising"*).

...a way to engage in a proven process that has an objective, an outcome, and can be duplicated and repeated.

Now that I've gotten that off my chest, let me elaborate on why I wrote *Asking about Asking.*

It really began several years ago during a conversation with my friend Jim Whitt. As we were getting acquainted he asked if my thoughts had been recorded in a book. After I responded in the negative, he exclaimed "Kent, you owe it to your audience to leave them with more than just a memory of what you have to share. They deserve to be able to go back and reference the insights you so readily offer. Your book will provide them with such an option."

Until then I had never *seriously considered* a book with my name on it. The idea of authoring anything of significance was something reserved in my mind for others. People like Jim who was already a published author. Jim's suggestion that someone like me had something of value to write in permanent form was totally unexpected.

But Jim planted a thought in my mind that day. And little-by-little the truth behind his proclamation became evident to me.

I began to think that I *might* write a book.

I began to think that I *could* write a book.

I began to think that I *should* write a book.

I began to think that I *would* write a book.

I began to think that I *must* write a book.

And, to state the obvious, I did write a book. (If you're not pleased with the result, please don't blame Jim. He can be held responsible for the *motivation* behind this book, but please don't punish him for the *content!*)

My intent in writing is to help others become better equipped for success in fundraising than I was when I got my start. I'm hopeful that others will be spared from making some of the many mistakes that I have made. More specifically, I'm writing:

- ◆ to remove fear from the solicitation equation;

- ◆ to equip the person whose fundraising reputation overshadows his actual experience;

- ◆ to help folks get past "no;"

- ◆ to instill the joy of a job well done in those actively engaged in the philanthropic quest;

- ◆ to correct the notion that "all of the truly great fundraisers are the 'big-time professionals;'" and

- ◆ to take a task that seems insurmountable—if not impossible—and break it down into steps that are manageable, achievable, and even enjoyable!

But, before going further, let me make a candid confession: *I'm not a great fundraiser.*

> I'm not a *great* fundraiser.
>
> **warning!**

No, I'm not a *great* fundraiser. I am a fundraising professional. I've been recognized by my peers as 'outstanding' in my chosen field. I can raise money—and lots of it. But the only truly *great* fundraisers are *volunteers*. People who willingly do things they don't *have* to do.

I'm not a *great* fundraiser, but I know some who are. These women and men are passionate about their cause. Volunteers like Robin Ballenger, Jim Pritchard, Betty Kane, John Mihm, Mary Ann Hille, Steve Turnbo, Clydella Hentschel and others. I could share lots of impressive tales of their fundraising exploits, but I'll have to save their stories for another book.

I'm not a *great* fundraiser, but I help lots of ordinary individuals become extraordinary fund finders. These are often people without great positions; without great possessions; without great power. But they have a wholesome degree of dissatisfaction with what *is*, and an unwavering determination to achieve their vision for what *can be*.

I'm not a *great* fundraiser, but I dedicate this book to that eager *volunteer* who wishes to become one. And I'm glad you decided to join me on this journey to master the art of Conversational Fundraising.

I'm not a *great* fundraiser, but I offer these ideas to the executive director who desires to better equip her board members to fulfill their duty of funding the mission of the organization they love.

I'm not a *great* fundraiser, but I devote the pages that follow to the development director who aspires to train others to successfully ask for gifts...and gratefully receive the response—whether positive or negative.

One more note. All of the stories you will read here are true. They have been verified as completely as possible. But in some cases, to honor the privacy of the individuals involved, the names used are fictitious.

As you read along, if you find a story that sounds like you—but has another name attached to it...it probably *is* you! In any case, I'd love to hear from you. Maybe you can update me on the rest of the story (what has happened subsequently), or find that it wasn't you at all.

Perhaps you're in better company than you realized.

And finally, I'm not a *great* fundraiser, but the act of writing this book has made me a better one.

I'm on the pilgrimage with you.

And the journey begins now.

On the very next page.

Section A—Introduction

IN THIS SECTION

I n our best work as fundraisers, we do a lot more *Asking about Asking*—than just asking for the gift alone. This section lays the foundation of basic concepts upon which the heart of the book is built. It addresses the sense of panic felt by the volunteer who has accepted an assignment for which he has no relevant experience. Next it equips fundraisers with ways to overcome these fears. The importance of strategically seeking large gifts is emphasized along with an outline of common terms used in the fundraising profession. The last chapter in this section reveals how essential it is for gift seekers to have confidence in the organization for which funds are being raised. This section is intended to be used and reused as a guide and coaching tool for those who are actually engaged in person-to-person gift solicitation.

In fundraising, 'the ask' refers to a direct request for a contribution from a specific prospective donor. For example, "George, would you donate $1 million for the new Boy Scouts campground?" Anyone who has ever made 'the ask' knows it can be a big deal. And the anxiety that goes with making 'the ask' isn't limited to requests for philanthropic support. The same dynamics are at play anytime a 'high stakes request' is made, such as:

◆ proposing for marriage;

◆ requesting a raise;

◆ seeking a promotion;

◆ pursuing a business investment;

◆ applying for a bank loan; or

◆ soliciting a sales order.

As you begin to evaluate these tense moments we all face, notice that they often revolve around some kind of 'ask'. The principles outlined herein apply to any serious appeal. But this book is focused on the request for charitable contributions.

So, the first topic we'll explore is the anxiety that accompanies 'the ask'.

Cast of Characters:

There are lots of examples and illustrations included in the book to illustrate a given practice or scenario. To assist in the reader's understanding, the following fictitious 'Cast of Characters' is used repeatedly:

Executive Director:	Michelle Gardener
Development Director:	Bart Buffington
Prospective Donors:	Katie and Jason Rutherford
Katie's 'peer':	Monica Springer
Katie's employer:	ABC Corporation
Jason's 'peer':	Aaron Skinner
Jason's employer:	Self employed
Nonprofit Organization:	Healthy Hearts Early Childhood Education Center
Campaign theme:	No Boundaries
Campaign purpose:	New school building
Campaign goal:	$10 million

our cast

Chapter One

Stage Fright?

IN THIS CHAPTER

···→ Asking for a gift—doing it right

···→ The joy of asking

···→ Revolutionize your asking

···→ My reward as a writer

C all it 'stage fright' if you like, but one of the most common fears among fundraisers is *actually asking for a gift*. And it's understandable why people are so apprehensive - it's done wrong more often than it's done right:

◆ The wrong people are involved.

◆ The relationship is not yet established.

◆ The process is mishandled.

◆ The prospect isn't ready to be asked.

◆ The preparation is insufficient.

◆ The promised results are uninspiring.

◆ The follow-up is missing.

And, while fundraising is an *im*precise science – there *is* a method to the madness. In fact, when properly handled, there's nothing to be mad about! One of the greatest joys in human relationships is asking

...someone you know
...to do something you've done
...to help others in need
...for a cause you are passionate about
...with their precious resources
...knowing they will be sincerely appreciated, and
...realizing the true joy and satisfaction they will experience because of the gift.

So, what's not to like?

For your own answer, just ask one of the countless staff and volunteers around you who have stumbled through the gift solicitation process. Listen to their experiences. See how their stories compare with the list above. You'll hear tales that will...

◆ bring you to tears,

◆ cause you to scratch your head,

◆ make you laugh,

◆ tempt you to pull your hair out, or

◆ make you swear not to ask anyone for a gift again. *Ever!*

But keep asking, and you'll find some real pros whose stories will...

◆ stir your soul,

◆ inspire your mind,

◆ motivate your next move, and

◆ awaken your desire to go forth and do likewise!

This book is their story. It's a story of ordinary people doing rather ordinary things in an extraordinary way and getting exceptional results. I call it Conversational Fundraising.

Conversational Fundraising will revolutionize your asking. Not just asking for charitable contributions...but *all* your asking!

Simply put, my hope is that this book will *equip, inspire* and *encourage* you.

"How so?" you may ask.

First, I desire to *equip* you to be more effective in your asking and provide you with tools you can actually use *every day*.

Then, my ambition is to *inspire* you to ask more boldly and confidently than ever before. It doesn't matter whether it's a $12 million foundation request to build that new community center, or an invitation for a friend to sponsor you for one hundred dollars at the Boy Scouts golf marathon.

And third, if I am successful, you will be *encouraged* in all your asking. Encourage, as defined by Merriam-Webster Online, means to "inspire with courage, spirit, or hope: to hearten, urge, stimulate, or foster."

My greatest reward, as a writer, will be to hear from you about your own implementation of Conversational Fundraising...

◆ Knowing that you are *heartened* by your early success in asking for philanthropic support.

◆ Learning that you are now *eager* to go out and ask others.

◆ Seeing that you have been *stimulated* to lift your own horizons.

◆ Realizing that you are *comfortably* asking someone for their most generous gift ever.

To Recap

Plan of Action

◆ What is your *biggest obstacle* to soliciting major gifts?

_____

◆ What *change in behavior* do *you* need to make to overcome this obstacle?

_____

◆ *Who* can come alongside and support you in this change?

_____

◆ *When* will you take the first step?
___/___/___ @ ___:___

Chapter Two

Larger Gifts

IN THIS CHAPTER

- ‑‑‑▶ Why ask for larger gifts?

- ‑‑‑▶ The 80:20 Rule

- ‑‑‑▶ The gift chart and levels of giving

- ‑‑‑▶ Looking for $1 million gifts

W hy ask for larger gifts? Because *everyone wins* when donors maximize their giving.

To better grasp the idea, picture your family gathered around the brightly lit tree on Christmas morning. You made a choice to give each child either a 'token' gift—or a 'generous' one. You readily did the latter. Now, simply contrast in your own mind the impact of your choice to give generously rather than reluctantly. How does this look through the eyes of the child? From the perspective of the other family members? And what about the effect your decision has on how you view yourself?

Pareto's Law

Vilfredo Federico Damaso Pareto was an Italian economist, sociologist, and philosopher born in 1848. Pareto's research revealed that 80 percent of the wealth belongs to 20 percent of the population. Pareto's Law, or the famous 80-20 Pareto Principle, was further applied to suggest that:

◆ 80 percent of the output results from 20 percent of the input,

◆ 80 percent of the consequences flow from 20 percent of the causes, and

◆ 80 percent of the results come from 20 percent of the effort.

In charitable giving this has historically been expressed by 80 percent of an organization's donations coming from 20 percent of those who contribute. Within the last two decades we have seen this shift to 90:10 for some organizations, and even 95:5 in some larger campaigns.

What this means is that, whether the ratio is 80:20 or 95:5, an overwhelming majority of the dollars will come from a relatively small number of donors. Therefore, if we are to reach the goal in an aggressive fundraising campaign, it will require that we succeed first in securing a *small* number of very *large* donations before seeking a large number of small gifts.

Stated another way, there simply are not enough $1,000 gifts available to take the place of a $1 million contribution.

We become more complete persons when we practice lavish generosity. In the same fashion, larger gifts made to a charitable organization are uplifting, inspiring and rewarding to the asker, the organization, the clients (needy children, for example) and, perhaps most importantly, to the donor.

Consider, for example, a campaign to raise $10 million.

Sample Gift Chart*

Leadership Gifts

1 gift of	$1,500,000	for a total of	$ 1,500,000
1 gift of	$1,000,000	for a total of	$ 1,000,000
3 gifts of	$ 500,000	for a total of	$ 1,500,000
6 gifts of	$ 250,000	for a total of	$ 1,500,000
11 gifts		totaling	$ 5,500,000

Major Gifts

12 gifts of	$ 100,000	for a total of	$ 1,200,000
18 gifts of	$ 50,000	for a total of	$ 900,000
36 gifts of	$ 25,000	for a total of	$ 900,000
66 gifts		totaling	$ 3,000,000

General Gifts

72 gifts of	$ 10,000	for a total of	$ 720,000
84 gifts of	$ 5,000	for a total of	$ 420,000
106 gifts of	$ 2,500	for a total of	$ 265,000
106 gifts of	<$ 2,500	for a total of	$ 95,000
368 gifts		totaling	$ 1,500,000
445 Gifts		Totaling	$10,000,000

* Notice that the Leadership and Major gifts categories constitute 17% of the donors, who contribute 85% of the dollars. Conversely, the General gifts category comprises 83% of the donors who give 15% of the dollars.

I want to draw your attention to three points of reference.

You will notice that

◆ Ten percent of the goal will come from one *leadership gift* of $1 million.

◆ About 13 percent of the goal will come from twelve *major gifts* of $100,000.

◆ Another 7 percent of the goal comes from seventy-two *general gifts* of $10,000.

Please soak-in this principle:

To succeed in a $10 million campaign we must make an intentional decision to *not* look for $10,000 donations (until near the end of the solicitation phase).

principle

The general gifts category requires 368 gifts totaling $1.5 million. The largest gift in this category is $10,000. Such a donation would ordinarily be considered a 'big gift' for this organization.

It might be exciting, fun, motivating, exhilarating...even easy to solicit $10,000 gifts. But seeking gifts of this size *too early* can actually cause our campaign to *fail*. Here's why: We have a tendency to find what we're looking for and a similar tendency to *not find* what we're *not looking for*.

Leadership **Level** gifts are those at the *top* of the gift chart and make up 55 percent to 60 percent of the total.

Major **Level** gifts are those in the *middle* of the gift chart and make up approximately 30 percent of the total.

General **Level** gifts are those at the *bottom* of the gift chart and make up 10 percent to 15 percent of the total.

finition

The problem lies not in locating gifts of $10,000, but rather in soliciting $10,000 gifts from $1 million donors!

When it *is* time to seek $10,000 contributions it will be challenging enough to find the seventy-two that are required by the gift chart. It can be tempting to think, "It's too difficult to find a $1 million donation. I can replace that $1 million gift by raising more gifts of $10,000."

Unfortunately, adding one or two zeroes to the *number* of gifts won't get us to our goal.

We must add the zeroes to the *amount* of the gift.

Stated differently, we must *stop* looking for $10,000 gifts and instead we must *start* looking for a gift of $1 million.

Seriously!

You've heard the old adage, "If you keep doing what you've been doing, you'll keep getting what you've been getting." You're not reading this book so you can keep getting the same old results you're familiar with. You have worthy reasons to begin getting different results. It's your mission... you're feeding hungry children, sheltering homeless families, protecting battered spouses and other equally inspiring services. You must do what you haven't been doing so your mission can reach *more* people. And impact *more* lives!

Stark Reality
To raise $1 million through $10,000 gifts will require *one hundred times the effort!* And that's just not possible.

practical tip

If you have to raise $1 million you must first determine how to go about it. The scenario we're using has defined a 'big gift' as one that is $10,000 or more. Now consider how hard you presently work to generate one big gift of $10,000. And if we take the approach of seeking the same size gifts to reach the fundraising goal, you will have to work one hundred times as hard to raise ninety-nine additional gifts of $10,000 in order to reach the $1 million goal. Perhaps with great determination, discipline and diligence some 'fundraising superstar' could do so eventually. But this is extremely unlikely.

No matter how determined, disciplined, and diligent you are, it's simply not possible for one person to increase their activity by one hundred fold. You can do the math from here. Let's put the extra zeroes somewhere else.

> The bad news is you just can't keep doing what you've been doing. But the good news is you won't keep getting what you've been getting.
>
>  practical tip

Today, you're raising one gift of $10,000 for a total of $10,000.

If our activity is increased ten fold, we could raise ten gifts of $10,000 for a total of $100,000. Or, with a one-hundred fold increase of activity we would generate one hundred gifts of $10,000 for a grand total of $1 million. To add two zeroes to the number of gifts obtained would be truly miraculous. But that's not even conceivable!

> **Stark Reality**
>
> You *will* find some $10,000 donors while seeking million dollar gifts. But you *will not* find any million dollar donors while seeking $10,000 gifts! (And you won't find one hundred donors of $10,000 either!)
>
>  practical tip

Our solution is, instead of adding zeroes to the number of gifts, add the zeroes to the gift amount. To make this shift calls for a much different *effort*. It's not the same *activity*. And fortunately, it's not the same *result*.

By redefining our target as $1 million gifts, and refocusing our activity on donors capable of giving $1 million gifts, we can reframe our work in a way that leads to success.

What if... What if we had a big enough vision to identify a $1 million problem in our nonprofit organization? *What if* we took that problem to our supporters, and looked for a $1 million solution? *What if* nine supporters only gave one-tenth of this amount ($100,000) and one caught the big vision and gave $1 million? Now we have $1.9 million! And, I assure you this will not require 190 times the effort that was required to secure one gift of $10,000.

It's important to realize that as an organization grows its service, its reach, and its significance - it must also grow its donor base. Therefore we must constantly be *renewing, replacing,* and *"requipping"* (my new word) our staff, volunteers, and donors.

> *"Requipping"* is to equip again, but differently than the original. It is to apply new thinking to old problems in such a way as to generate dramatically different results than were achieved in the past.
>
> finition

It would take a small army of fundraisers to secure one hundred gifts of $10,000. But a trained, motivated, focused, disciplined force of one can identify, cultivate, and solicit one gift of $1 million! This will not happen every day. But it can be done.

Getting personal

So what about you? Will you take the 'zero challenge'? *You decide.* You decide how many zeroes to add to your definition of a 'big gift.' One... two...three? (But if you take the challenge, *'none'* is *not* an acceptable answer.) Stop looking for gifts of $10,000 and start looking for gifts of $1 million. In the process, some $10,000 gifts will still find you. And that's okay. We will always gratefully receive $10,000 gifts. We'll still carefully steward contributions of $10,000. We'll graciously and sincerely thank $10,000 donors. But courageously embark on your pursuit of $1 million gifts. *You go find* the larger gifts, and let the smaller gifts find you.

To Recap

Plan of Action

◆ *Will you* take the 'zero challenge'?
   ❏ Yes
   ❏ No

◆ *How many zeroes will you add* to your definition of a 'big gift'?
   ❏ One
   ❏ Two
   ❏ Three

◆ *Name your top three prospects* for a 'big gift' (as redefined):

   _____
   _____
   _____

◆ *Write an action plan* with detailed steps for approaching these three funders. You might want to come back and revisit this plan after you finish reading this book.

Chapter Three

Gift Terminology

IN THIS CHAPTER

···→ Definition of terms

···→ Gift size

···→ Perspectives in giving

Before going any further, let's define a few terms:

◆ 'gift of convenience'

◆ 'gift of obligation'

◆ 'impulse gift'

◆ 'go-away money'

◆ 'token gift'

◆ 'transformational gift'

◆ 'gift of significance'

A 'gift of convenience' is simply that; it's convenient for the donor to make the gift, requires little thought, and takes less effort than other giving options.

When making a 'gift of obligation,' there is a sense that one really has no choice in the matter. Because of the donor's wealth, public standing, membership, etc. they feel obligated to contribute. Unfortunately, there's really not much satisfaction for such givers. They have simply fulfilled an obligation.

'Impulse gifts,' similar to 'gifts of convenience,' are hastily made. This is what happens when someone is emotionally moved by an introduction to the charitable cause, responds on the spot, and immediately feels like they have addressed the problem. My friend Jim Pritchard once pointed out "The guy that gives $1,000 in response to a letter in his mailbox feels just as good as if he had given $10,000, had he only been asked for it." Jim's observation has been validated countless times in the actions of others. This is just another example of giving on 'impulse.'

'Go-away money' is the term associated with dismissing a fundraiser by simply writing a check. If, early in the conversation, a modest check is presented, it can be an indication that "I'm really busy (or distracted) with other things right now...I have more money than time...and it's easier for me to write you a check and get you to go away than continue to listen to you." Read on and you'll learn how to avoid the 'go-away money' syndrome.

A 'token gift' results from a desire to be included on the list of contributors, but not holding enough passion for the project to give at the higher level of one's capability. Oftentimes the 'token gift' is the donor's way to avoid becoming a 'conspicuous absence' from the donor list, while having no concern about where the donor's name appears on that list.

'Transformational gifts' are defined by their size in relation to the annual budget of the organization. These gifts are so large that they truly transform the charity's future.

A 'gift of significance,' however, is judged through the eyes of the donor. It is a contribution that is truly significant from the viewpoint of the one making the gift. Such a gift requires careful contemplation. It must be decided upon with adequate background information. And it holds much meaning for the one who signs the check. *Significant!*

As grateful fundraisers, we endeavor to view every gift *from the donor's perspective.* Therefore, we see each gift—whether large or small—as significant *to the donor.* This is why we say that every gift is gratefully received. And carefully stewarded.

This is not the same as discussing gift size. It is true that larger gifts add up faster. They move the organization toward its goals at a more rapid pace. Big gifts tend to get more public attention and acclaim. But it is our opportunity—as real fundraising pros—to celebrate gifts of significance in ways that encourage other constituents to be intentional about their own giving as well.

> *Whatever we praise, recognize and reward we will see more of.*
>
> —unknown

To Recap

Gift Terminology—Plan of Action

◆ Which terms do you need to *remove* from your fundraising vocabulary?

_____

_____

_____

_____

◆ What terminology will you *add* to your thinking and everyday usage?

_____

_____

_____

_____

Chapter Four

My 'Big 3'

IN THIS CHAPTER

····→ Why relationships matter in fundraising

····→ Donors' passion for the mission

····→ Making a difference in the long-term

····→ The finest people in the world

T o be successful in fundraising requires a variety of qualities and characteristics.

Over the years I have noticed three elements that are essential to true, lasting success. I call these my *'Big 3'* and they require that fundraising activities be:

1. *Relationship* focused,

2. Centered on the organization's *mission*, and

3. Oriented toward the *long-term*.

Indeed, there are numerous people who approach fundraising without regard for these emphases, but the results they achieve will either be temporary or unsatisfactory. Or both.

The chapters that follow explain these essentials in detail. They also reveal why my *'Big 3'* emerged as such, and how you can create a legacy of fundraising success by adopting them as your own.

My 'Big 3': #1 — Relationships

There is an enormous difference between a transaction and a relationship.

Transactions are characterized by their efficiency. If you're interested in transactions, go to Kmart or McDonald's. They specialize in transactions. You're in and you're out. Get what you want and be gone. It's quick, it's easy and it's over.

But approach fundraising like that and you can expect to end up with 'transaction-sized' results. Something such as a Dollar Menu or the Blue Light Special.

By contrast, we are focused on philanthropic decisions that involve thousands, tens of thousands, hundreds of thousands or millions of dollars. Those don't occur at a drive-thru window or the checkout stand. Nor do they occur through direct mail, Twitter or the telephone, although each of these media has its respective place in your development plan.

Focus on the *relationship*.

People new to fundraising often have a misconception that they're going to somehow show up in a dramatic, charming fashion and easily walk away with big contributions from 'those rich people.'

The reality is that people don't like to be treated like commodities. And it's the same whether rich or poor. Meaningful relationships take time. Soliciting a major contribution can't be done on impulse. And approaching it that way will insure a short-lived fundraising career— whether as a volunteer or a professional.

This is the paramount reason for including a prospect's peer as an integral part of the cultivation and solicitation process. Each of us has an abundance of personal relationships. Each of those relationships was formed in a unique setting. And who can know all of the purposes for which a given friendship has come into existence? It seems to me that there are just two alternatives here (back to my sense of the profound!):

Either...

　　　...the relationship exists for *some purpose*...

　　　...or the relationship exists for *no purpose.*

Since I'm one of those people who believe that things do not simply happen at random, there must be a purpose for the relationships in our lives. And if this is so, I choose to believe that the purpose is high and noble. So why wouldn't I willingly explore whether such a purpose might be served by an organization with a mission inspiring enough for me to have volunteered?

Major donor solicitation begins like any other relationship; getting to know the person behind the gift. In order to know someone, you have to meet them. Despite the popularity of Facebook, email and text messaging, the best way to get to know someone is to meet face-to-face.

One of the things I love about being active in charitable organizations is that I have the privilege of meeting and working with the finest people in the world—*people who do what they* don't *have to do.*

Nobody *has to* make a charitable contribution.

Nobody *has to* volunteer.

Those who do contribute and volunteer are, by definition, the finest people in the world. And these are the people from whom fundraisers solicit large contributions.

Before going any further in this endeavor, commit yourself to taking the necessary steps to establish the relationship first—and then seeking the gift. A world of rewarding relationships awaits you!

My 'Big 3': #2 — Mission

The second of my foundational emphases is to understand that the support is for the benefit of the mission.

♦ If I'm the executive director, it's about the mission. It's not about me.

♦ If I'm the board chair, it's about the mission. It's not about me.

♦ If I'm the director of development, it's about the mission. It's not about me.

♦ If I'm the fundraising volunteer, it's about the mission. It's not about me.

♦ And if I'm the program officer, it's about the mission. It's not about me.

I think you get the idea. We're raising money to advance the mission. So it's imperative to keep the conversation centered on the mission. Why the organization exists. Who we help. What difference we make. And how we can do more.

My observation is that every charitable organization begins with a boatload of passion. And it's that passion which propels a nonprofit organization from start-up to sustainable. But, so often the very people who eagerly stepped forward as members of the founding board seem to have forgotten why they are involved when it is time to seek the financial support of others.

My 'Big 3'

Effective fundraising is all about:

1. *Relationships (not transactions)*

2. Organizational mission (not individual needs and desires)

3. Long-term objectives (not today's crises and pressures)

practical tip

Much of my work involves equipping, or "requipping," board members of such organizations. I love to get acquainted with these leaders by asking this question, "If we woke up this morning and Healthy Hearts Early Childhood Education Center no longer existed, *who would care?*"

The responses they give illustrate persuasively the impact for which the agency was created. I can then rapidly understand why the nonprofit organization is worthy of support. It's truly inspiring.

The follow-up question goes something like this, "You've identified others to whom the charity is important, but what about *you? Why do you* care so much that *you* would sacrifice *your* precious time and invest *your* limited dollars to move this mission forward?"

Now it gets personal. People astound me with their very compelling and touching reasons for supporting such causes. As I listen, I am moved—sometimes to tears—with the passion and dedication within the governing board. My job becomes easy. I simply give people permission to tell others their story and ask for support. This is what it means for fundraising activities to be *centered on the mission.*

Mission statements are designed to readily communicate the primary purpose for which an organization exists. While the goals, strategies and plans of an agency address the 'what' (how many, how often, how fast, how high, etc.)—it is the mission statement that really expresses the 'why.' And people ultimately fund the 'why'—not just the 'what.'

When a request for funding is firmly based on the mission, it alleviates the apprehension associated with "asking someone to give *me* money." That sounds self-serving and people are, understandably, reluctant to ask this way. Instead, the request for a gift to support 'the deprived children in our community' puts the focus right where it belongs—on the needs of the constituents we serve, not the 'needs' of the organization or the asker.

If we are to solicit support for an organization we must understand the mission well enough to inspire such support. And, while it is impossible for any one person to have a full understanding of every dimension of a nonprofit organization's history and operation, it *is* realistic to expect

fundraisers (paid or unpaid) to be able to articulate *why* the organization
was created, what its successes and challenges are, and how it intends to
address emerging needs going forward.

When preparing to introduce prospects to the work of your organization,
it's important to think about the kind of things people want to know
about nonprofits. In my experience, the basic questions generally revolve
around these topics:

◆ What do you do?

◆ Whom do you serve?

◆ How much does it cost?

◆ What are your successes?

◆ What are your failures?

◆ How many people are impacted by your work?

◆ Who else is involved (board members, volunteers, funders,
   advisors, etc.)?

A well written case statement helps answer such questions and is a great
tool for fundraisers, volunteer and staff alike. Its use will be paramount
when cultivating potential supporters.

Guidelines for Case Statements

Every organization needs to articulate its nature, purpose, and principal
objectives in a concise and consistent manner. This is best accomplished
through the use of a document called a case statement. The case
statement describes the organization's cause and why it deserves
philanthropic support. When developed properly and used strategically,
it has a dramatic and powerful impact on the future of the organization.
According to Hal Seymour, a case statement must "Catch the eye, warm
the heart and stir the mind."

The key components of a case statement are:

- ◆ The type of service you now provide.

- ◆ Your future objectives.

- ◆ Why your activities and programs are important.

- ◆ Who benefits from the organization's activities (value to society).

- ◆ Your philosophy, your operation and your mission.

- ◆ The nature and extent of your financial needs.

- ◆ What will make the organization stronger and more effective.

- ◆ How the funds you seek will help your organization serve more effectively.

- ◆ What mandates propel your organization forward.

The case statement is a valuable tool for obtaining consensus on the organization's story, recruiting volunteer leadership, testing the market, and creating fundraising materials.

Eight essentials the case statement should include:

- ◆ The organization's history.

- ◆ The problem to be solved.

- ◆ The opportunity to be seized.

- ◆ The proposed solution— including key strategies.

- ◆ The organization's unique role (its track record of success).

If a sixth grader can understand your case statement, you're on the right track!

practical tip

◆ Plans and goals.

◆ The leadership structure.

◆ How to make a gift.

My 'Big 3': #3 — Long Term

Finally, successful fundraising is all about the long term. There are a variety of practices that could be successfully employed if all we needed to do was survive until the end of the month (or year). However, those very practices are counter-productive if the organization intends to survive (or even thrive) well into the future.

By way of example, I'm reminded of an educational organization that decided they absolutely had to raise $9 million by the end of the calendar year. If this did not happen, they claimed the future of the organization would be irreversibly jeopardized. Their primary tactic for motivating people to respond was fear, followed closely by shame. Needless to say, the philanthropic community did not embrace the challenge. And those who did make large gifts did so out of the wrong motivations. I would venture to say that twenty years later none of the donors who responded to the abovementioned challenge still support the organization.

Another dimension of the long-term objective is our treatment of those who donate and those who do not.

Donors have confided in me unbelievable stories of a lack of gratitude for gifts they made. The biggest mistake is the failure to say a simple 'thank you'. One foundation officer told me about a community-wide initiative that funded over sixty organizations. Gift acknowledgements were extremely slow in coming. So the foundation sent individual requests to the donees, asking them to send a 'thank you' letter. After waiting another sixty days a full 20 percent still had not bothered to acknowledge the gift. This kind of neglect doesn't play well for the long term. If you were the donor, how open do you think *you* would be to the next request for funds?

Then there is the expectation of perpetual funding. A corporate gifts officer shared the story of receiving calls from past grant recipients, in a demanding tone, asking, "When will our next check arrive?" without any such funding commitment having been extended. That sounds like a technique to assure that the agency won't survive for the long term.

Conversely, I had the privilege of working with an organization that respectfully asked for funding from a foundation prospect, but was turned down. Appropriately, a letter acknowledging the decline was sent and contact was made later to learn the reasons behind the 'no' decision. This polite, professional exchange continued off and on over a period of thirteen years before a gift was ever received. And when it came, the commitment was for $100,000 per year for three years. This was a very large grant in the scope of the donee, and a significant first gift from the viewpoint of the donor. Can you imagine how different the story might have ended if the gifts officer had given in to his initial impulse to 'throw a brick through the window' (see Chapter Twenty-Seven, *Listening and Responding* when the earlier requests had been declined)?

There are five key concepts to be underscored here:

1. The first answer we receive is rarely the last answer.

2. The first gift we receive need not be the last.

3. Decisions change.

4. People change.

5. Positions change.

Best practices suggest that we treat everyone like major gift prospects. When it's time for donors to make a big gift decision, they should feel eager to give their philanthropic support because of the way you've interacted with them previously.

If you will keep these considerations in mind they will enable you to remain oriented toward the long-term and succeed both in the present and the future.

To Recap

My "Big 3"—Plan of Action

Relationships

◆ *Who* do you need to become acquainted with for the purpose of creating a relationship with your organization?

_____

_____

_____

◆ *Who* do you have a relationship with that should be viewed differently (less transactional & more relational)?

_____

_____

_____

◆ What will be *your first step* in making this change?

_____

◆ *When* will you take it?

___/___/___ @ ___:___

Mission

◆ Does your nonprofit organization's *mission* or *vision statement* need to be revised, shortened or replaced?
❑ Yes
❑ No

◆ Is your *case statement* up-to-date, concise, clear and convincing?
❑ Yes
❑ No

◆ Is your fundraising more...
- ❑ *Person* centric? or
- ❑ *Purpose* centric?

◆ What needs to change *first*?

_____

◆ *How* can *you* appropriately *prompt* this change?

_____

◆ *When* will you get started?

___/___/___ @ ___:___

Long Term

◆ In *which area* does *short-term thinking* hamper your organization's progress?

_____

_____

◆ *How* would *long term thinking* alter the messages you convey to your constituents?

_____

_____

◆ *Who* should be involved in recasting the vision or reframing the discussion for your organization?

_____

◆ *What* is the next step in the process?

_____

◆ *When* will you take this step?

___/___/___ @ ___:___

Chapter Five

Speaking with Confidence

IN THIS CHAPTER

- ···→ Getting your message heard

- ···→ The two impressions a speaker will make

- ···→ Budgeting your time in donor calls

- ···→ Practice makes perfect

- ···→ The Cycle of Confidence

U p to this point, much of our attention has centered on *what* we communicate to our donors and prospects. In this chapter we give attention to *how* we communicate.

In the philanthropic arena, confidence is essential to both parties. On one hand we have the fundraiser's confidence. On the other is the confidence of the contributor.

Let's start by addressing the confidence of the solicitor.

When first approaching a prospective donor, the fundraiser might have a tendency to be timid. This hesitancy can best be overcome by having clear, concise printed materials and a well-developed plan to guide the presentation.

In order for a message to be heard, it must be clear, concise and understandable. One of the greatest challenges we all face in communication is relaying sufficient information without delivering too much.

Adapt your case statement, promotional materials and spoken messages to 'Kiplinger Style.' What I mean by this is to pare your content down to the bare essentials.

Whether spoken or written, be diligent to compress your message! Use pictures, graphs, and printed materials to communicate quickly and concisely. Speak in concrete terms (not vague).

The reason it's hard to shorten a message is because speakers always have vast stores of information of utmost importance to themselves. Their

---

Kiplinger Style

Kiplinger is a Washington, D.C.-based publisher of business forecasts and personal finance advice, available in print, on line, audio, video and software products (Kiplinger.com).

Its best-known publications are *The Kiplinger Letter*, a weekly business and economic forecasting periodical for people in management and the monthly *Kiplinger's Personal Finance* magazine.

—Source: wikipedia.org

Kiplinger's trademark style consists of highly condensed information in bullet-point format for a quick, 'bottom-line-oriented' read.

subject matter is highly relevant, motivating and even life-changing (to the speaker, even if to no one else). Thus, it's natural to ramble on at great length. Oftentimes the speaker will 'lose the audience' along the way. Sometimes it's because the speaker runs out of time before getting to the main point. Other times it's because the main point is obscured by the vast amount of minutiae surrounding it. In either case, the message isn't caught by the audience, resulting in a communication failure.

Perhaps you can relate to my friend, Casey Church, who sat through one such session and later declared, "The only way he [the speaker] could have said less was to have spoken longer!" That sounds like an

---

Need More Help?

Overcome fear; develop personally and professionally by doing the following:

- ◆ Practice with a friend or colleague.

- ◆ Enroll in a public speaking course.

- ◆ Practice with a frequent donor.

- ◆ Volunteer to speak on behalf of another cause.

- ◆ Practice with an occasional donor.

- ◆ Join Toastmasters International.

- ◆ Practice with a prospective donor.

Dr. Ralph C. Smedley, founder of Toastmasters, is quoted as saying, "The unprepared speaker has a right to be afraid."

practical
tip

exaggeration, but I sat through the same session and I think Casey's summary is right on target.

You have the opportunity to determine which impression your audience walks away with. If you err, let it be on the side of speaking too briefly, rather than too long. People are always tolerant of being 'released' ahead of schedule. But no one appreciates being 'held hostage' longer than expected.

> Whenever you speak, people will leave with either of two impressions: They will have had their interest piqued, and want to hear more, or they will have heard more than they cared to and will avoid another encounter.

 practical tip

This same dynamic is at work in one-on-one meetings. When you visit with a prospect, strive to create a thirst for more information. Don't leave the prospect feeling annoyed for having spent too much time listening to your monologue.

Here are my guidelines for managing your meeting time. Let's say the appointment was scheduled for thirty minutes. Budget your time as follows:

4 minutes for introductions and pleasantries

8 minutes (or less) to deliver the heart of your message

8 minutes to answer the prospects' questions

1 minute to make your 'ask', whatever the request is (at this point, you are 2/3 of the way into your appointment)

5 minutes for the response/negotiation

2 minutes to recap and schedule your next meeting

28 Minutes Total
(this allows you to finish ahead of time—or take two additional minutes to deal with any contingencies that may arise)

Now that we know to keep our message concise, let's focus on delivering that message with confidence.

If the fundraiser doesn't feel confident about the cause, the prospect is unlikely to contribute at a meaningful level. Somehow—through our body language, facial expressions, tone of voice and manner of delivering the message—we tend to 'telegraph' our attitudes to our audience. This will happen whether the outlook is positive or negative. To be effective in gift seeking, staff and volunteers must be well enough informed to be confident that the gift requested will accomplish the intended purpose...if the donation is made.

Arrange your schedule so you are available to stay longer than agreed. But *only do this at the request of the prospect*, not because *you* took more time than planned.

We have discussed the solicitor's confidence and how that affects her delivery of the message and the donor's reception of the same. Now let's

Practice Makes Perfect!

Master the Art of Conversational Fundraising by practicing these principles. As you practice during your cultivation and solicitation calls, the principles will turn into skills. With more familiarity, the skills will become habits. Soon the habits will become 'second nature' for you. Shortly you'll be teaching others how they, too, can engage in Asking about Asking.

Principles ⇨ Skills ⇨ Habits ⇨ Second Nature

address another dimension: the donor's confidence in the charitable organization.

The only reasonable source for such confidence is *knowledge.* The most convincing knowledge is that which comes from outside the organization. Prospective funders want to be sure their gift will prove to be a wise investment. They will examine the stability of the nonprofit organization's finances before committing significant funds. Such an examination often begins at the *formal* level, by looking at official reports and documents.

Step one may be inspecting the organization's IRS Form 990 on GuideStar. org. In addition, requests will likely be made for the most recent financial reports (internal validation) and the previous year's audited financial statements (external validation).

Inevitably, these reports will give rise to additional questions and/or concerns. It is at this moment that *informal* sources of validation become priceless. A simple inquiry to a friend (or the friend of a friend) will either resolve financial concerns or put the prospect on high alert.

It is for this reason that the volunteer structure for major fundraising campaigns includes a finance committee. The assurances of volunteers who are competent in financial matters—and independent of the board of trustees—will speak volumes to prospective funders. The funders' confidence in the project will increase dramatically based on a simple endorsement from a trusted community leader.

The IRS reports that, as of December 31, 2009 there were 1,238,201 nonprofit, charitable organizations registered under Section 501(c) (3) of the Internal Revenue Code. The vast majority of these nonprofit organizations are legitimate organizations working hard every day to achieve their philanthropic mission. They rely on charitable contributions from individuals, businesses and foundations to conduct their programs.

There are several ways donors can obtain third-party validation of these organizations. The most common source of verification, however, comes from the charity itself. Each organization produces a wide array of documents and reports each year and sends them to donors and prospects.

Due to the foresight of several visionaries, *A Donor Bill of Rights* was created many years ago (see Appendix B). If you examine these ten rights carefully, you will notice that each one creates a basis for trust between prospective donors and the nonprofit organizations they are asked to support.

Trust leads to confidence. Confidence leads to generous giving. Generous giving prompts donor stewardship. And donor stewardship stimulates trust. It's a self-perpetuating cycle.

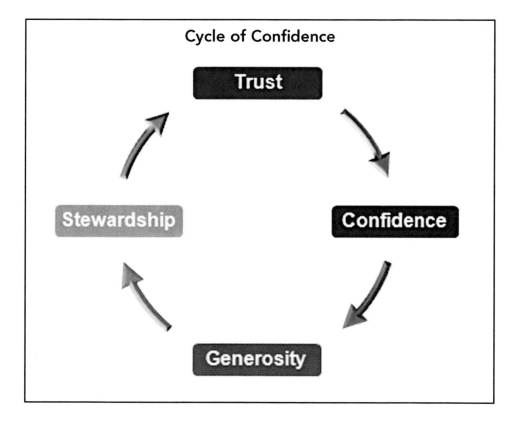

Cycle of Confidence

I would encourage each staff member and volunteer who reads this book to evaluate their organization's practices in light of the Donor Bill of Rights. Be sure these rights are actually adhered to by your organization. If you find any shortcomings, correct them.

This proactive approach will enhance your organization's reputation and demonstrate that it can be trusted.

To Recap

Plan of Action

- ◆ *What* needs to be done to boost *your* confidence as a solicitor?
  _____

- ◆ *Who* can come alongside and support you in this change?
  _____

- ◆ *What* needs to be done to boost your *prospects'* confidence?
  _____

- ◆ *When* will you take the first step?
  ___/___/___ @ ___:___

Section B—The *Purpose* of Asking

IN THIS SECTION

T his section gives an overview of the gift-seeking process. Beginning with step one, exploring donor interest, it guides readers through the process of cultivation, solicitation and appreciation. Fundraisers are encouraged to practice Conversational Fundraising and thereby understand donors' personal wishes. The focus is on preparing a gift proposal that exactly reflects the donor's desires and intentions. The specific strategies in this section equip fundraisers to manage the two risks most likely to derail a gift request.

Effective fundraising is not a guessing game...it's an asking exercise. In Chapter Ten you'll read more about the perils of guessing, but for now, let's agree that there are plenty of benefits to asking...and dangerous pitfalls when we fail to do so.

Cultivating and soliciting major gifts occur frequently during a capital fundraising campaign. We should recognize that the focus is different when we are discussing the overall campaign (INternally) than when we are speaking to specific donors (EXternally). The fundraising campaign *must never overshadow* the donor.

What I mean is this: From the organization's viewpoint the *campaign* is about the big picture. It's about...

- ◆ our project,

- ◆ our timeline,

- ◆ our vision,

- ◆ our programs,

- ◆ our goals, and

- ◆ our clients.

And that's not wrong. Leaders of the nonprofit organization must manage the effort from an overall standpoint.

But when it comes to soliciting gifts, it's a different mode altogether. *Gift seeking* is all about the *donors*. It's about...

- ◆ their needs,

- ◆ their vision,

- ◆ their timing, and

- ◆ their preferences.

At the organization level, it's all about our mission. But in the individual solicitation, it's all about the donor. Be always vigilant not to switch these emphases. To do so will wreak havoc in both realms.

One of the ways to keep focused on the donor's priorities and pressures is to learn exactly what those issues are. Rather than seeking this information elsewhere and getting out-of-date or secondhand input, don't guess...ask.

When we guess, we are hindered by our limited knowledge, personal filters, extrapolations, and assumptions. There is an automatic tendency to formulate answers to questions about others based entirely on our own experiences.

Asking, on the other hand, acknowledges that the answers to certain questions must come from *someone else.* From the other person...the one who actually knows the answers. No guessing!

In serving the needs of donors, we must set aside the faulty practice of guessing and replace it with the informative art of asking. In doing so, we will choose from various types of questions such as:

◆ exploratory,

◆ clarifying,

◆ rhetorical,

◆ educational,

◆ defining, and

◆ informative.

Asking for charitable donations is always enhanced with thorough exploration *before* 'the ask.' And pre-request inquiries are just as valuable for other solicitations as well, such as:

◆ "Would you join our board?"

◆ "Would you chair the fundraising campaign?"

◆ "Would you lead our strategic planning task force?"

Never guess when you can ask.

practical tip

In Chapter Six you will encounter *The 10 Step Staircase,* a method to effectively prepare prospects to respond to solicitations, regardless of the request.

Chapter Six

The 10 Step Staircase

IN THIS CHAPTER

 ···→ Is it a step or a leap?

 ···→ Pursuit of a relationship rather than a transaction

 ···→ Substituting a process for one-time events

T hose who are engaged in fundraising are eager to hear donors say "Yes" when asked for their philanthropic support. But experience tells us that it rarely happens the first time we show up. In fact, if we hear 'yes' too soon it may be an indication of a premature request (see Chapter Nine, *Two Risks to Avoid*). Successful fundraising requires a *process* and *patience*.

Think of gift solicitation like standing at the foot of a staircase and wishing to get to the second story. It would be nice to get there in one giant step, but that is neither possible nor ideal. Just as the staircase requires taking one comfortable step after another, soliciting major contributions consists of a number of activities—each taken in order. Of course, there are times when we are in a hurry and take the stairs two at a time. It can be done, but—if we are not cautious enough—we may slip...fall...and have to start over.

The steps in the charitable solicitation staircase might look something like *The 10 Step Staircase* illustration on the next page.

You just agreed to chair a $10 million capital campaign. Picture yourself standing at the foot of a staircase. At the top of the stairs is a door that represents a $1,500,000 grant from the William and Inez Barrows Goode Foundation. You want to pass through that door and secure a leadership gift from the foundation. But you've never done this before.

Where do you start?

My suggestion is to simply take the first step.

Each of these steps involves many details. And the process is described step-by-step on the pages that follow. But there's no need to worry about *all* that is involved in taking the *last* step. We just have to get started with step 1, getting acquainted.

Depending on the circumstances, some of the steps may already have been taken. Or you may be able to combine two or even three of the steps into one meeting. Other times, it may be necessary to go back and repeat some of the steps.

But, generally speaking, step 2 comes *after* step 1 and *before* step 3, etc. Since each person, organization, project and situation is unique, it's advisable to modify the plan when needed. But let me caution you not to make *arbitrary* leaps over the steps on the staircase.

Before probing each of the tasks represented by the steps on the staircase, I thought it would be helpful to look at the overall 'climb' for an understanding of what lies ahead.

The main points to be emphasized here are:

The 10 Step Staircase

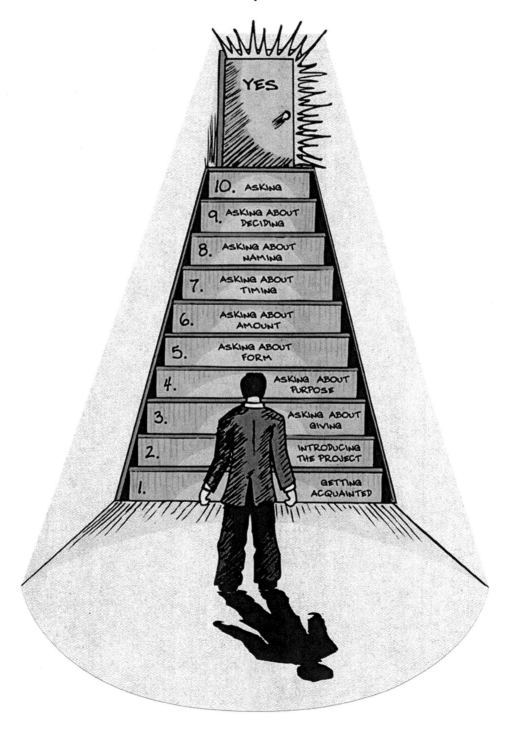

◆ It's a climb up the stairs, not a jump to the top.

◆ It's a relationship with a person, not a transaction with a machine.

◆ It's a process, not a one-time event.

◆ It's about the donor, not about the asker.

◆ It's about patience, not about haste.

◆ It's deliberate, not haphazard.

◆ It's delicate, not forceful.

To Recap

Plan of Action

◆ Which steps are you inclined to skip?

10. Asking

9. Asking about Deciding

8. Asking about Naming

7. Asking about Timing

6. Asking about Amount

5. Asking about Form

4. Asking about Purpose

3. Asking about Giving

2. Introducing the Project

1. Getting Acquainted

◆ Are there any steps that cause you to feel paralyzed?

   ❑ Yes
   ❑ No

◆ If 'Yes,' which steps?

   10. Asking

   9. Asking about Deciding

   8. Asking about Naming

   7. Asking about Timing

   6. Asking about Amount

   5. Asking about Form

   4. Asking about Purpose

   3. Asking about Giving

   2. Introducing the Project

   1. Getting Acquainted

◆ Develop an *action plan* for disciplining yourself to ascend *The 10 Step Staircase* with *one specific prospect.*

◆ *Evaluate* the results.

◆ *Revise* and repeat.

Chapter Seven

Asking ... to Learn

IN THIS CHAPTER

- ┈➔ The reason for asking

- ┈➔ Being intentional with your questions

- ┈➔ Spontaneous inquiry

- ┈➔ Searching for buried treasure

I learn a lot more when I'm *listening* than when I'm *talking*.

The reason for asking questions is to learn. Another purpose for inquiry is to instruct. This method was perfected by the Greek philosopher Socrates. He developed a method of teaching based on asking questions to stimulate critical thinking. There can be any number of other purposes for asking questions, but in this chapter we'll focus primarily on *Asking to Learn*.

Let's begin with an examination of this most basic reason to ask.

One of the central concepts behind Western civilization is the importance of education. I like the way Daniel J. Boorstin said it. "Education is learning what you didn't even know you didn't know." There seems to be a natural inclination built into most of us that gives us the mistaken notion that 'I already know all there is to be known.' Wrong! And sometimes, because we are intelligent, we have to discipline our minds to recognize that there's more to be known. Much, much more.

One of my college roommates, Wayne Yust, pointed out a pet peeve of his—the misuse of the word 'obviously.' One day Wayne mused that people often say something like "Obviously, that's not the correct answer." Wayne went on to explain, "What seems so 'obvious' to one person must not be 'obvious' to another person, or the other person wouldn't have come up with a different answer. Consequently the word 'obviously' ends up being used in a way that is an insult...albeit unintentional."

So in order to have true, meaningful conversation, we must get beyond what seems obvious. We do so by *Asking to Learn.*

If we are going to ask to learn, it will require just a bit of planning:

1. Determine *what* you want to learn.

2. Identify *who* you want to learn from.

3. Finally, formulate a question that will elicit an answer to illuminate your mind on the given topic.

One such experience for me involved a corporate executive with a stellar reputation in his field of business. He was generous with his personal resources and had enjoyed unusual success in raising his family. I did not know David Corts personally, but wanted to get acquainted and glean some of his life lessons. I decided to apply the three-step formula above as follows:

1. I wanted to learn tips for success in family and business.

2. David Corts was the source I wanted to learn from.

3. I had two questions for David:

   a. "What do you consider to be the greatest single factor behind your success in business?"

   b. "What have you done to keep your family relationships so strong?"

Next, I called David to ask if I could 'pick his brain' over lunch, and I would buy. As I look back on this experience today, I realize that my request was unusually bold. David was a top executive in a multinational corporation. I was nobody. The fact that he even accepted my call – much less joined me for lunch—is a tribute to his gracious character. Yet, I'm so greatful that I made that bold move those many years ago.

Rather than share all the success tips I garnered that day, let me say there were many, and I have adopted several for use in my own business and family. In addition, I gained a friend that day. We have shared many experiences together since then. To my amazement, David actually asked my opinion on a couple of issues that day. And, he even bought *my* lunch. What an unexpected treat!

The bottom line is: I intentionally asked to learn that day. I learned what I was seeking. But I gained far more than I could have dreamed during that brief lunchtime encounter.

I should point out, however, that some asking is less intentional. More spontaneous. For example, I once had a meeting with an elderly widow who had been very generous to the liberal arts college I represented. She had contributed thousands of dollars annually for many years to provide scholarships so that deserving but underprivileged students could attend this private school. Her husband had been equally generous during his lifetime. There were many years in which she donated more to the college than I *earned*. 'She must be extremely wealthy,' I thought.

Imagine my surprise when I arrived at her home for my first visit. I expected a grand estate—or a sprawling farmhouse at least. But instead, I found myself entering a very modest bungalow. To call it a 'humble abode' would be an overstatement.

As I climbed the two steps to her front screen door, I heard an old, but strong, voice say, "Come right in...I'm not getting up to open the door for you."

And that's just what I did. As my eyes adjusted to the dim indoor light after leaving the bright summer sun, I saw her sitting in an old rocking chair in the corner of the living room. Victoria wore a faded duster and was working diligently with something in her lap. "What are you working on today?" I inquired.

"Oh, I'm just doing some mending," she replied, holding up a needle with thread and a couple of pieces of fabric.

After taking a closer look at her handiwork, I was almost speechless...she was sewing a patch on a patch on a washcloth. That's right. A patch *on a patch!*

Now, I knew she could have purchased the local department store if she wanted. She was a major shareholder in two banks, and owned large acreages in at least two states! So you can understand why I found it baffling that she was using her time to patch a worn out patch on a worn out washrag.

I just had to ask, "Mrs. Plummer, there are any number of things you could be doing with your time. Why are you mending that old washrag?"

As she replied, I learned far more than the answer to a simple question. She told me, "I'm patching this cloth so I don't have to go buy a new one. That way, I'll have more money for scholarships to help more kids attend the Bible School (as she called it)." End of answer. Case closed. And to her, it must have seemed really obvious. By the time I left it had become obvious to me, too.

I began to realize that Victoria Plummer's large, generous, frequent donations *didn't* come from the abundance of her possessions. She was giving sacrificially. She was *willing to want,* if it meant making life's goals a little more attainable for someone else. Another generation of 'young folks' as she called them.

I'm glad I asked Victoria what she was doing—and why. I could easily have guessed, assumed or surmised. But I could never have *known* what I know today if I hadn't asked Mrs. Plummer for a simple explanation.

After our brief visit, when she invited me to stay for lunch, there was *no way* I was going to offend Victoria by suggesting that we drive into town for a meal at the local diner. *No!* She had brown bean soup and cornbread on the stove, made from scratch that morning. Indeed, I enjoyed a simple meal that hot summer afternoon. And it was made all the more delicious by my realization that we were enabling her to "help more kids attend the Bible School."

As it turned out that day, I had a true *feast!*

Sometimes I think fundraising is like the search for buried treasure. We have been told—convincingly—the treasure exists. We know it's out of sight—buried. Our task is to find it. If we're digging in a place where the treasure *isn't*, we want to know as soon as possible...so we can dig somewhere else. However, just because we don't strike 'pay dirt' with our first spadeful doesn't mean the treasure isn't there. The most successful treasure hunters are dedicated enough to keep digging until they reach the treasure—or confirm that it is *not* here. In fundraising we say you must 'dig where the gold is.' It involves both the science and the art.

To Recap

Plan of Action

◆ Think about your prospective funders. *What* would you like to learn from them?

◆ *Who* would you want to learn from?

_____

◆ Write *three questions* you could ask that would teach you what you want to learn.

1. _____

2. _____

3. _____

◆ Decide *when* to call and schedule your meeting.

___/___/___ @ ___:___

Chapter Eight

Drafting a Proposal

IN THIS CHAPTER

··· ➔ Put it in writing

··· ➔ The essential elements of a gift proposal

··· ➔ How the word 'DRAFT' can become your best friend

To refresh your memory, the theme of this book involves asking major gift prospects essential questions about their potential donation *before* asking for a gift decision. I recommend that you condense your request. Put it in writing. Draft a gift proposal. Let me explain.

When a request for a contribution is put in writing, it forces us to be specific about all the essential elements of 'the ask.' These elements are:

    1. Name of the donor,

2. Name of the donee,

3. Date the commitment was made,

4. Amount of the contribution,

5. Dates the contribution will be made,

6. Specific purpose of the gift (programs, endowment, construction, equipment, etc.), and

7. Naming considerations, if any.

DRAFT Gift Proposal

To:	Katie and Jason Rutherford
From:	Healthy Hearts Early Childhood Education Center
Date:	February 11, 20xx
Amount:	$1.5 million (over three years)
Purpose:	No Boundaries campaign
Naming:	Betsy Armstrong Activity Room
Fine Print:	The donation will be fulfilled by stock transfers during each of the next three years. Our facility naming policy requires the board to give final approval to this naming request.

Approvals:

_____   _____   _____
Katie Rutherford   Date   Jason Rutherford

There can be lots of other details pertaining to a gift or pledge, but they are not relevant until a *decision* has been made to actually go through with a gift. So think in terms of negotiating these other specifics *later*.

The primary value of a written gift proposal is that it helps you, as the gift *seeker*, stay focused on what you are requesting, and it helps gift *makers* understand exactly what they are agreeing to do.

This is not to suggest that the writing of a proposal *dictates* the donor's decision, rather it serves to *clarify* and communicate the charitable intent.

I cannot overemphasize the value of clear, written gift documents. For years I worked as CFO of a charitable organization and more times than I can count, questions arose about the exact purpose of a gift that had been given years earlier. Sometimes the answers were as readily available as pulling a folder from a file cabinet. Other times the answer was so obscure, it required seeking out court documents from the estate of the long-since-deceased contributor.

In a sense, a well-crafted gift proposal is like the two sides of a coin. One side provides value immediately. The value of the other side is realized much later.

Eventually this proposal will be agreed to by the donors and affirmed by their signatures. Before that happens, however, there is a lot of work to be done. And that's where my next strong recommendation comes in: the use of the word 'DRAFT.'

Stamp the word 'DRAFT' in large letters across the top of the proposal. This practice is *huge*. It gives everyone involved complete freedom to make changes. It communicates, "I'm not here today to ask you to 'sign away your life.'" It says, "A time is coming when you will be asked to formalize your gift commitment. But today is *not* that day. Today, let's talk." I have put numerous persons (askers and givers alike) at ease by simply announcing, "I am committed to working with you on this proposal until it *exactly describes* the gift you want to make." And then we continue the process of '*Asking about Asking*' until we get the proposal exactly right.

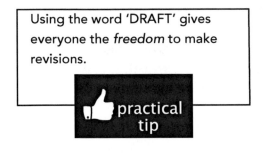

Using the word 'DRAFT' gives everyone the *freedom* to make revisions.

practical tip

The proposal can be as simple as the half-page version shown on page 56, or it may be like the formal gift proposal example in Appendix E. Use your own discretion to choose the right tool for the job. But put this advice to use in your own work. I predict that it will improve communication, focus the discussion, clarify important details, and remove some of the stress that you feel as a fundraiser. It will also alleviate uncertainty within your gift prospect.

I believe you will find this to be a very rewarding practice. And someday, years hence, an accountant in an obscure back office will "rise up and call you 'blessed'" upon finding all possible questions about an ages-old gift answered on a single sheet of paper.

To Recap

Plan of Action

- ◆ Create a simple *sample proposal* for your organization.

- ◆ *Personalize* it to correlate with an upcoming 'ask.'

- ◆ Conduct a role play with a colleague to become more familiar and comfortable with your process.

- ◆ Evaluate the process and refine/repeat as necessary.

- ◆ Schedule a meeting with the prospect.

Chapter Nine

Two Risks to Avoid

I n asking someone else for a decision on any matter, there are two basic risks to avoid. I refer to these as the risk of early *rejection* and the risk of early *acceptance*.

The risk of early *rejection* involves someone saying "No" to our request before they have enough information (or connection) to make a fully informed decision. Similarly, the risk of early *acceptance* results in a quick "Yes" decision—but at a much lower level than what their true potential might be. In other words, we get an answer right away but it is made in such a hasty fashion that it minimizes the ultimate value of the decision. Let's look at an example and consider specific ways to minimize these two risks.

Amanda Andrews is a retired school teacher. She has minimal connection to the programs of Healthy Hearts Early Childhood Education Center. Her financial support has been intermittent and modest. She volunteers for special programs about twice every three years. Several of Amanda's closest friends are deeply involved with Healthy Hearts.

One of those close friends is Mary Ellen Goldman, who recently agreed to serve on Healthy Hearts' campaign cabinet. An informal assessment suggests that Amanda might be a prospect for a leadership level gift to the campaign – in the range of $250,000 or more over a three-year period. At the last cabinet meeting Mary Ellen agreed to approach Amanda regarding the campaign. In preparing to fulfill her assignment, Mary Ellen has identified several risks she wants to avoid:

◆ When invited to learn more about the project Amanda may say "No."

◆ Amanda could say, "I've already heard about their upcoming campaign, and I'll just put a check in the mail. We really don't need to meet."

◆ Amanda may indicate that she "doesn't really have time to get involved with another charitable cause."

What are some similar objections you have heard?

Mary Ellen's objectives are to:

◆ Fully inform Amanda about the purpose and background of the campaign;

◆ Adequately motivate Amanda to become involved financially; and

◆ Help Amanda come to a decision that she will be happy about over the long term.

Mary Ellen has already taken the first step by arranging for Amanda to attend an introductory meeting with Healthy Hearts' executive director, Michelle Gardener. So the question is, "How can they avoid the risks of early rejection and early acceptance when they meet?"

We've already begun to manage the risks by *identifying* them. This can easily be accomplished by conducting a pre-meeting planning session. It is always advisable for the call team to meet in person, prior to the cultivation (or solicitation) meeting, to prepare for a successful outcome. In the planning session, we will anticipate the inclination for Amanda to either say a hasty "No" or volunteer to "drop a check in the mail as soon as I return home."

When making cultivation or solicitation calls, use a 'call team' consisting of:

- *The CEO of the nonprofit organization*, and

- Someone who is a *peer* to the prospect.

(See Chapters Fifteen and Sixteen.)

 practical tip

The best strategy now is to outline the risks when meeting with Amanda, and offer alternatives that will minimize or avoid the likelihood of her saying "Yes" or "No" too soon. Experience tells us that we might employ the following approach:

When Mary Ellen and Michelle meet with Amanda, and as soon as the initial introductions have been made and the pleasantries are behind, Mary Ellen can say something like this: "Amanda, Michelle and I are so excited about Healthy Hearts' campaign. And we're pleased that you have taken time for today's meeting. In case you're worried about us asking you for a gift today, let me put you at ease. That's not why we're here. We would love to have you donate to this project at the appropriate time, but that's much later. Today what we want to do is bring you up-to-date on Healthy Hearts' activities and get your advice on how you may wish to be involved."

What you will notice in Mary Ellen's announcement is that she indicates what today's meeting *is* about and what it *is not* about. In my experience, this kind of announcement has a tendency to put everyone at ease: the prospect, the peer, and the CEO. We announce what the path forward will look like, which takes away almost all of the fear. People fear the unknown. So we alleviate this fear by making the unknown ("What do they want from me today?") known ("We want to bring you up-to-date and get your advice").

Another comment that helps manage the donor's expectations should be interjected at some point during the cultivation call. It goes something like this, "At the appropriate time, we'd like to prepare a written gift proposal for your consideration. When we do, I want to be sure it is exactly right for you. And my commitment is to work with you until every detail meets your complete satisfaction."

What we're communicating is:

⬥ This process is important enough for us to be intentional.

⬥ We're interested in Amanda's interests, desires and goals ("...exactly right for you.").

⬥ We're sensitive to her timeline ("At the appropriate time...").

⬥ And we're prepared to be patient ("...work with you until...").

When we focus on the donor's needs it becomes easy for her to trust us enough to cooperate in 'rightsizing' her involvement through a carefully crafted gift proposal.

As you think about ways to minimize the risks of early *rejection* or early *acceptance* in your life, what hopes and fears do you have? What forms might the 'rejection' take? What are some different forms of 'acceptance' you wish to skillfully manage?

To Recap

Plan of Action

- ◆ What types of early acceptance do you encounter?

    _____

    _____

- ◆ Identify steps you can take to reduce or eliminate the risk of early acceptance.

    _____

- ◆ What forms of early rejection have you experienced?

    _____

- ◆ Identify steps you can take to reduce or eliminate the risk of early rejection.

    _____

Section C—The *Process* of Asking

IN THIS SECTION

W hile providing a proven process for securing major gifts, Section C covers the discovery process, focusing on the fact that when we guess about a donor or gift, we are almost always wrong. The section equips readers to become more effective fundraisers by engaging prospective donors in meaningful conversations. Readers will build their proficiency in asking the right questions at the right time and listening effectively to donors. These chapters include specific questions, phrased in precise ways, which a fundraiser can ask while cultivating donors' involvement. These questions are helpful not only during gift solicitation, but are part of a conversation with the donor from the very first meeting.

The idea of soliciting charitable contributions as a process, versus a onetime event, was illustrated with *The 10 Step Staircase* in Chapter Six. Now I want to highlight some of the other concepts that are essential to successful gift seeking. As you proceed, be ready to immediately implement what you learn or refine your existing practices if need be. But don't overlook the fact that you are taking a journey.

Be prepared to take as much time as your prospect needs. You'll want to get moving, but don't rush.

Here are nine commitments we want to make to each other before conducting a solicitation or cultivation call:

◆ We will not guess when we can ask.

◆ We will not say 'no' for the donor.

◆ We will be straightforward.

◆ We will faithfully observe the *Donor Bill of Rights* (see Appendix B).

◆ We will comply fully with the AFP Code of Ethical Principles and Standards (see Appendix A).

◆ We will *refuse* a gift or pledge if it is offered in a meeting we established based on *not* asking for money.

> **Stewardship Principle**
>
> The Stewardship Principle states that the work of a fundraiser is to help donors achieve *their* philanthropic goals...*not* to attempt to determine their charitable goals *for them.*
>
> **principle**

◆ We will *not* request a contribution before fully exploring the donor's interest in each facet of the proposed project.

◆ We *will* ask for a gift or pledge when the prospect is ready to be asked.

◆ We will *disengage* from the prospect who informs us that they have no interest in our mission (see the *Stewardship Principle* in the sidebar above).

The topics outlined in the following chapters will position you for greater success than you have ever experienced. It's the idea of getting out of the business of guessing and assuming. And getting into the business of *asking.*

Chapter Ten

Assuming and Guessing

IN THIS CHAPTER

- ···→ The problem with guessing and assuming
- ···→ The discipline of asking
- ···→ Why we choose to *not* ask
- ···→ Carefully crafting your conversations
- ···→ Asking for permission

I have seen countless mistakes made in fundraising. In fact, I have made most of them myself at one time or another. Perhaps the most natural mistake would be for us to assume or to guess.

The problem with assuming or guessing is that it is time consuming, counterproductive and eventually frustrates everyone involved. These behaviors will eventually steer gift solicitors down dead-end streets as they pursue the false premises that always emerge when people speculate.

When we refrain from asking we will make assumptions in numerous areas such as:

Scarcity	vs.	Abundance
Resistant	vs.	Willing
Reluctant	vs.	Eager
Stingy	vs.	Generous
Apathetic	vs.	Interested
Later	vs.	Sooner
Guarded	vs.	Open
Aloof	vs.	Friendly

The very act of asking is, in itself, a certain kind of discipline. In a lot of ways it's much easier to simply guess. It seems that we all have a natural inclination to guess about things we're not certain of. But guessing is a very risky business. And if you look closely you'll notice that even the most experienced guessers aren't really very good at guessing *correctly*.

And therein lies the problem.

Assume—to take for granted or without proof; suppose; postulate.

Guess—to arrive at or commit oneself to an opinion about something without having sufficient evidence to support the opinion fully; or, an opinion that one reaches or to which one commits oneself on the basis of probability alone or in the absence of any evidence whatever.

When involved in a *simple* transaction it really doesn't matter if we guess *in*correctly. When you step up to the counter at your local hamburger joint the server may guess that you want ketchup, onions, pickles and mustard on your burger. And if he guesses wrong, the fix is rather simple. Not a big deal. Right?

When the stakes are greater— as in the case of a major gift decision—why would we even consider *not* asking? Here are some of the excuses I have heard:

◆ "It takes too much time."

◆ "I will look ignorant if I ask about something so elementary."

◆ "I already have a 'pretty good idea' without asking."

◆ "This topic seems a little too personal for me to be asking about."

◆ "If I ask it may seem like I don't already know something I should."

◆ "I don't want to seem as if I didn't do my homework beforehand."

◆ Etc., etc.

These are some of the fears and concerns that will nag at the back of our mind, causing us to take the bigger risk of guessing.

How do people react when we ask the kind of questions recommended on these pages? My experience is that they realize and appreciate our *genuine interest*. They find a certain enjoyment in talking about themselves. Oftentimes they will learn something about themselves. Or organize their thoughts in ways they haven't done before. Or recall a happy memory that seemed to have been long forgotten.

A carefully crafted conversation, sprinkled with appropriate inquiry, can be the beginning of a trusting relationship or deepen an existing one. You'll notice a careful 'framing' of the questions we suggest. And please be alert to the difference between a blunt intrusion and thoughtful probing.

Early in my career I worked with someone who had an inordinate inclination to guess about things. No matter how simple the topic, Steve would guess (wrong) ten times rather than ask once. And he *always* got it wrong. We almost always do, but Steve had a real knack for making his wrong guesses painfully obvious.

As we were working on a difficult project one day, Steve began to guess about the details behind a complicated mathematical calculation that Donna, another of our coworkers, had made in preparing the annual budget. When I noticed what was happening, I simply asked, "Instead of guessing how Donna arrived at that figure, why don't you ask her?" It was as if I had just invented fire! An enlightened look came over Steve's face and he responded, "Sure, I can do that!" So, off he went to track down Donna—the only person who really knew the various elements to this complex equation.

A short time later Steve returned with the information we needed to proceed. After Steve relayed the answer I asked him, "How long do you think it would have taken you to guess until you got the correct answer?"

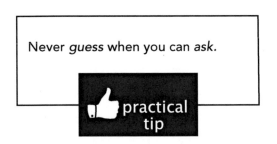

Never *guess* when you can *ask*.

practical tip

He instantly replied, "I think I could have spent the rest of my career guessing and still never have come up with the correct answer."

I think he was right. Not because of any lack of intelligence on Steve's part. It just reveals the reality that life's possibilities are virtually unlimited. And, when it comes to personal matters, I have found that the risks of guessing are indeed countless.

So let me offer my strongest recommendation: *Never guess when you can ask.*

You may have to discipline yourself in this regard in order to break old habits. But you will quickly find that your own 'conversation quotient' will rise dramatically.

If you're the least bit hesitant, let me suggest that you practice. Invite a friend to lunch by explaining, "I'm working to improve my conversational skills and would like to buy your meal today and practice with you. Are you game?"

In advance, write out four or five questions you would like to explore with your friend. Why not use some of the real questions we suggest throughout this book? Such as:

◆ "How did you become so successful in your career?"

◆ "How did you learn to give?"

◆ "What would you like your gifts to accomplish?"

◆ "How do you decide which projects to support with your own time and money?"

◆ "What are your top three charitable interests this year?"

◆ "What gift did you make that has brought you the most joy?"

◆ "Why?"

Be ready to listen. Be ready to learn. And be ready for your relationship to grow. It's inevitable.

Then when it comes time to actually make a cultivation call with a real, live donor prospect—if you're particularly hesitant to ask an important question—simply ask for permission first. "Could I have your permission to ask how you learned to be so generous?"

Certainly the possibility exists that someone may respond negatively to such a request for permission. But that has never happened to me. My experience is: When a polite request is made, with a genuine interest, and sincerity of purpose—people are happy to grant their consent. And they often will respond in a way that answers other questions that you might not even think to ask.

Sometimes the consequences of assuming and guessing are minimal. Other times they are enormous.

Pete Alonzo was one of those persons described in the book, *The Millionaire Next Door.* He maintained a very modest lifestyle and had acquired his wealth by years of hard work and extreme frugality.

Harley Drummond was an aggressive fundraiser, but was much better at telling than asking. He had been calling on Pete for many years, and was frustrated at his seeming lack of progress toward securing a large gift that Pete could easily make.

When I was brought into the solicitation process, I wanted to understand the background as fully as possible. So, I began to ask.

I asked about the prospect; his giving history, his preferences and priorities, his family and his plans for the future.

Then I asked about the previous attempts Harley had made to engage Pete. After some time I discovered several problems with the solicitation efforts. Rather than cover all of them at this time, let me illuminate the most serious.

Harley was aware that Pete's children were married and had families of their own, and that Pete lived by himself. Assuming that Pete's wife was deceased, Harley had repeatedly approached Pete with the proposition that he might make a sizeable gift to memorialize the mother of Pete's children. The sad reality was that the woman was not dead. They were divorced!

Needless to say, the naming gift never materialized. The fact that a gift of several hundred thousand dollars did transpire is almost miraculous. But there was a long season of 'repair work' necessary before a successful 'ask' could ever be made. Of course it's easy to see the problem now: one mammoth-sized assumption that could easily have been avoided with one or two simple questions.

Always ask. You'll save yourself immeasurable embarrassment and difficulty.

As we come to the end of this chapter I'd like to make an assignment. Consider it an investment in your professional development or an expansion of your skills as a civic volunteer.

Identify three people you would be comfortable with and schedule a time to practice asking some of the questions above. Or, even better, come up with your own set of questions. And ask away!

Take a friend to breakfast, coffee, lunch, dinner or dessert and see what happens. After you do this three times with different friends, evaluate your experience. Decide what you liked and what you didn't. What will you do differently next time? What will you repeat? At the end of your time together, ask your friend to give you some feedback:

- ◆ "How did you feel about our conversation today?"

- ◆ "Did I ask anything that made you uncomfortable?"

- ◆ "What suggestions do you have that might help me improve?"

To Recap

Plan of Action

- ◆ Identify areas in which you have a tendency to assume or guess.

  _____

- ◆ Write out your own questions to substitute for assuming and guessing.

  _____
  _____
  _____

- ◆ Practice asking these questions with a friend.

◆ Evaluate the outcome and revise as necessary.

◆ Practice asking these questions with a current donor.

◆ Evaluate the outcome and revise as necessary.

◆ Practice asking these questions with a prospective donor.

◆ Evaluate the outcome and revise as necessary.

Chapter Eleven

Conversation versus Confrontation

IN THIS CHAPTER

···→ Fundraising's negative connotations

···→ Victims of 'fundraising'

···→ On ramps and off ramps to the fundraising highway

A fter conducting an intense two-day board workshop, I was approached by a retired news anchor with this disclosure, "When you use the term 'Conversational Fundraising,' I just don't see the 'conversation' part. I would never converse with a friend in a social setting about any of the topics you outlined." I must admit that my initial reaction was to recoil as if I had suffered a direct blow! What was I missing? What was *he* missing? My mind was deluged with questions and possibilities that would take some time to sort through. Eventually, it turned out that this gentleman had actually given *me* a gift. His direct and somewhat caustic approach forced me to clarify some of my own thoughts and presumptions. And today you get the benefit of my pain.

Oftentimes when people hear the term 'fundraising,' a negative connotation comes to mind. For some, it involves the following image of a 'fundraiser'—a disheveled old man at a busy street corner, with a tin cup in one hand and a scribbled sign in the other. His unspoken plea is: "Hi! I don't have any money. You do. Give *some* of it to me."

Or a friend of mine in Las Vegas tells of a guy out on The Strip who holds up a ragged cardboard sign that says, "Why lie? I need a beer." At least he's honest! They're both 'fundraisers.'

Conversation—is an informal interchange of thoughts, information, etc., by spoken words; oral communication between persons; talk.

Confrontation—is to come face to face with, especially with defiance or hostility; or to come up against.

For others, the preconceived notion is only slightly worse. This time it involves an unshaven man with a mask over his eyes, a gun in one hand, and a canvas bag in the other. Oh no! Another fundraiser! The words he speaks are different from the first two, but the implied message is almost the same: "Hi! I don't have any money. You do. Give it *all* to me."

Of course, it's hard to find volunteers to play any of the roles outlined above. Who wants to be seen as the street panhandler? Or the hold-up guy? Nobody! And who wants to be approached by these characters? Same answer—no one! With these images in mind it's no wonder that people start backing away when it's time to assemble a team of volunteer gift solicitors.

What we've outlined above is a series of classic *confrontations*. And in some form or fashion, much of the fundraising that takes place in our society has a confrontational element to it.

Two reluctant parties come together almost by chance. A confrontational 'ask' is made. The monetary exchange may or may not take place. The parties go their separate ways. But neither is satisfied with the result.

Perhaps you have been the victim of a fundraising 'confrontation' yourself. If so, the last thing you want to do is participate in another such experience.

In place of the above, consider an entirely different scenario. You're relaxing after a hard day's work at a reception for the new Superintendent of the Metro Public School system. The room is full of your peers—people who are personally invested in the growth and success of the community. Someone you have known for years sits down across from you and asks that age-old greeting, "What's new with you?" You've just been drawn into a conversation.

What follows can either be purposeful or random. And it's usually up to you to decide. My suggestion is that you make the opportunity count for something. And why not make it count for something that really matters? For the benefit of your favorite charity.

My friend, Gail Perry, suggests that, in response to the question, "What do you do?" you might reply, "Do you want to hear about my vocation, or my avocation?" What a great lead-in to talking about your volunteer involvement!

The conversation might continue something like this: "I've been working on a project for Healthy Hearts Early Childhood Education Center. I have served on their board for the last three years. Nobody else does as much in our community as they do to equip kids for success in life. Have you ever been to their school?"

> The difference between a *confrontation* and a *conversation* is *permission*.

practical tip

That's a simple introduction, an invitation to chat, if you will. And, depending on the response you receive, it will either blossom into a full-blown conversation or fade away into disinterested nothingness. Either alternative is acceptable. If they're not at all interested in needy children in the local community you certainly don't want to force the issue. On the other hand, if they *do* have an interest in the topic, don't deprive them of knowing about the good work that is being done to help people with real needs.

The real distinction between conversation and confrontation is permission. In *confrontational* fundraising you forge ahead regardless of the prospect's interest and desires. But in *conversational* fundraising you only move to the next stage after obtaining the prospect's approval. This distinction is of utmost importance, for it will determine the degree of post-encounter satisfaction that will be shared by both parties. And whether the ultimate result is a decision to support your cause or not, you want to leave your friend feeling good about the journey.

The 'on ramps' to the Conversational Fundraising highway are paved with permission. And 'exit ramps' are freely available for any traveler who no longer desires to travel this road.

So, it's time for a bit of self-examination. How's your 'conversation quotient'? Do you have a need to control the outcome of every discussion you initiate? Or is there room in your mind for more than one answer to the questions you raise?

What if you're unsure about this approach? Then let me suggest that you simply take it for a test drive. Try it out with a friend. Then ask for feedback. "Was there anything about this conversation that was uncomfortable for you?" Or..."What could I do differently next time to make our conversation more enjoyable?"

To Recap

Plan of Action

 ◆ Write out your 'invitation' to engage someone with
    Conversational Fundraising.

   _____

   _____

   _____

◆ Try it out at your next social event.

◆ Evaluate your experience.

◆ Adjust and repeat.

Chapter Twelve

Choosing the Questions to Ask

IN THIS CHAPTER

···→ How to ask strategic questions

···→ Twelve tips for better questions

···→ Types of questions to use during fundraising calls

···→ Selecting the proper sequence for your questions

C hapter Thirteen outlines *The Essential Practice of Listening*, but before we can listen strategically, we must first ask strategic questions. What might those questions be? Certainly the selection of the right questions will vary from one prospect to the next, but there are some common themes to be considered as you prepare to call on prospective donors.

The sample *contact plan* in Appendix F has proven to be a useful tool in preparing the CEO and peer for meeting with a major gift prospect. Its greatest value lies in the way it stimulates our own thoughts about what might actually take place during the meeting.

As you prepare your contact plan, the first decision to be made is to identify the primary purpose for this meeting. Until the objective is clearly stated it is unlikely that the meeting will be truly productive.

Once you have zeroed in on the exact purpose for a particular meeting, you'll be ready to formulate the specific questions that should be answered before the meeting ends.

Remember; unless the meeting you are preparing for is Step #10—Asking, your purpose is to Ask about Asking, and the questions you choose should be designed to lead up to 'the ask.'

Here are twelve tips for your questions:

1. Pre-plan your questions by writing them out in advance (but be prepared to be spontaneous as well).

2. Formulate each question to address a single issue versus multiple issues.

3. Make every question concise versus rambling. Don't use long involved questions.

4. Avoid leading questions (those that begin or end with "don't you," "isn't it," "wouldn't they," etc.)

5. Practice rephrasing questions, if needed, for clarification.

6. Avoid ambiguous questions. These often lead to confusion or arguments.

7. Choose words that are clear and easily understood.

8. Resist the temptation to answer your own questions.

9. Formulate questions that are relationship building (versus fact-finding only).

10. Only ask questions for which you want an answer at this time (thus guarding against the risks of early acceptance or rejection). For instance, if you are just beginning to cultivate a prospective volunteer to serve as campaign chair, do ask, "Could we visit about your involvement with an upcoming project?" Don't ask, "Can you spare enough time to chair our next capital campaign?"

11. Ask questions that are thought-provoking. Consider what kind of thoughts and discussion your questions will stimulate.

12. Be sincere in the questions you ask. Have a genuine interest in the other person's answer—even if it is different than what you might have expected, hoped for, or intended.

There are three types of questions to consider as you decide what to ask in Conversational Fundraising:

◆ Rhetorical questions,

◆ Closed questions, and

◆ Open questions

Rhetorical questions are not generally asked for the purpose of obtaining an answer. Rather, they are statements posed as questions for the purpose of persuasion or stimulating the listener to think about what the obvious answer might be. They do not bring the expectation of a reply, but bring attention to the point being made by the speaker. Example: "Who could say 'No' to an opportunity like this?"

Be careful not to overuse rhetorical questions in this type of conversation. The main purpose for the questions we are describing is to learn about our prospects, rather than to persuade them about something.

Closed questions are those that can be answered either with a short phrase or a single word (such as 'yes' or 'no'). They generally begin with:

is, has, did, can, will or would. Closed questions give you facts, are easy to answer, take less time, call for a conclusion and may shut off discussion. Example: "Can we count on your support?"

Open questions invite longer answers and discussion. They begin with: what, when, where, which, how, or why and cannot be answered with a 'yes' or 'no.' Asking open questions invites the other person to think, remember or reflect. They prompt feelings and opinions. Example: "How did you come to that decision?"

Using Questions During a Cultivation Call

Use two or three closed questions at the beginning of a conversation. For example, "did you take a family vacation this summer?" "May I offer you something to drink?" "Who painted this picture?"

When you move to the heart of your conversation, use open questions to get the prospects to think and share insightful information. Such as, "How would you like to be involved in our campaign?" Or, "What range of gift should we be talking about?" This will allow you to learn more about the prospect's wants, desires, needs, problems and priorities.

Use rhetorical questions only on an occasional basis to emphasize a point. For instance, "Can you imagine the impact this project will have on our community?" Be careful not to make false assumptions or be presumptuous with your rhetorical questions. These could be offensive to the listener.

At the end of the call, use a closed question to summarize your

Choose Your Words Carefully

Writer Mark Twain, in a letter to his friend, George Bainton, gave this advice about selecting the right terminology in communication: "The difference between the almost right word and the right word is really a large matter—it's the difference between the lightning bug and the lightning."

practical tip

progress and to obtain permission for taking the next step; for example, "May I draft a proposal for your review?"

Here are eight questions that can be adapted to fit almost any Conversational Fundraising situation:

1. "May I introduce you (to the executive director, mission, programs, etc.)?"

2. "Could you ever see yourself (being involved, supporting, serving, etc.)?"

3. "When would be the appropriate time (for you to join our board, for your pledge decision, etc.)?"

4. "What would have to happen for you to say 'yes' (to a gift request, invitation to serve, etc.)?"

5. "Would you consider (a gift of $350,000 over three years)?"

6. "How would you like to be thanked (for your gift, service, etc.)?"

7. "Who else should we be talking to (about being involved)?"

8. "Would you introduce us?"

Adapt these questions to fit your prospects and to address the purpose of a given meeting.

Another question that can be extremely useful is "What are you hearing about _____?" This question gives the other person an opportunity to express their own thoughts through the voice of others. Such as, "What have you been hearing at the country club about our capital campaign?" People will almost always give an answer. Sometimes it isn't because they hear others talk about the topic, but because they have thoughts of their own and are willing to relay them as if from someone else.

Other questions you might want to include in your collection of ready-to-use inquiries are:

◆ "What do you think?"

◆ "How did you come to feel so strongly about...?"

◆ "What would be your advice about...?"

◆ "How do you feel about our proposed new program?"

As you listen to a prospect's answers, you may need to engage the other member of your call team by asking him or her to comment on what is being said. For example: "Janice, what do you think?" Or, "Would you agree with that?" "What would be your advice?" "Can you see how this might work out?"

Be alert to the sequence of your questions. Asking the right question at the wrong time can be worse than not asking the question at all. For instance, picture yourself asking the 'who else' question during an introductory conversation. The non-donor's response to the 'who else' question differs significantly from the response that you would receive from a recent donor. The former is likely to suggest the name of someone you can talk to 'instead of me.' The latter, however, will immediately think of others whose gifts can assure the success of the overall project—thus leveraging the 'return on investment' that the donor has just made.

As mentioned earlier, strategic listening flows out of asking strategic questions. Careful consideration of the questions to be asked will dramatically increase the likelihood of hearing the answers needed to make a properly crafted gift proposal.

To Recap

Plan of Action

◆ Evaluate your present use of questions. Which type of questions do you tend to *overuse?*

    ❑ Rhetorical
    ❑ Closed
    ❑ Open

◆ Which type of questions would you say you *under*use?

    ❑ Rhetorical
    ❑ Closed
    ❑ Open

◆ *Write four questions* you can use in your next cultivation call.

    1. _____

    2. _____

    3. _____

    4. _____

◆ *Practice* asking your questions and evaluate the results.

◆ *Make changes* as necessary.

◆ Put your revised questions to use the next time you meet with a prospect for the purpose of Asking about Asking.

Chapter Thirteen

The Essential Practice of Listening

IN THIS CHAPTER

---→ The most important part of asking

---→ How to listen more effectively

---→ Listening with your ears

---→ Listening with your eyes

---→ Listening with your heart

I n the previous chapter we introduced a variety of strategic questions that, when asked, enable fundraisers to practice strategic listening. In the next chapter we will deal with ways to respond to the donor's comments, concerns and objections. In this chapter we elaborate on ways to listen actively and truly come to understand your prospect.

After preparing and asking purposeful questions, it's time to be quiet and listen. This may be the most important part of asking. Indeed, if we are not deliberate about listening, there is really no purpose to be served by asking.

Listen *actively* to the prospects' responses. What are they saying? What are they *not* saying? What does this say about them? What does it mean for your charitable organization? What does it mean for the project?

Some tips regarding listening:

> *If you wish to know the mind of a man, listen to his words.*
>
> —Johann Wolfgang von Goethe

   ◆ Demonstrate a sincere interest in what the other person is saying.

   ◆ Interrupt only if needed to seek clarification of what is being said.

   ◆ Don't get caught up in formulating how you will relate your experiences to the other person.

   ◆ Be patient. If someone wants to speak at length in response to a question, allow them the time to do so.

   ◆ Seek to go beyond hearing to truly understanding. For example, if you hear, "That was a hard lesson for me to learn," ask a follow-up question such as, "How so?" or "How did it make you feel when that happened?" etc.

   ◆ Be careful not to become a distraction to the person you're listening to. If you hear something so important that you need to write it down, don't just pull out a pen and paper as if you were a news reporter. Say something like, "What you've said is so important that I'd like to write it down—if you don't mind." This is another example of permission-based communication versus intrusion-based tactics (see Chapter Eleven).

Hone your listening skills. Pay attention to the words you hear, but also be alert to the other person's body language. What is being said? What is being left *unsaid?*

Learn how to read and interpret the *meaning* the speaker is communicating (with words and by other means). Communication experts tell us that only 7 percent of the meaning in a message is contained in the words alone. Another 38 percent comes through the tone of voice. Yet a whopping 55 percent occurs by observing body language!

To be sure, listen with your ears. Hear the words that are said. Notice the tone of voice the speaker is using. Be alert to the volume, be it a whisper or a shout. Observe the pace of speech.

Also, practice the skill of noticing and understanding nonverbal messages. Listen with your eyes. Observe the other person's body language. If they're leaning back, it could be an indication that they're bored. If their arms are crossed, they are probably not receptive to your message. If they are not being particularly attentive, there may be something distracting their concentration. If so, consider asking if you should reschedule your meeting for another time.

Finally, listen with your heart. Develop your intuition to discern if the conversation you hear seems right. Does the message ring true?

Be attentive. If there is an objection, do not assume what the cause or issue may be. Don't be reluctant to address any topic that raises questions in your mind. Instead, ask.

Use nonverbal signs to indicate that you understand. Nod and smile to demonstrate you are paying attention. Ask for clarification or affirmation to keep yourself and the speaker engaged in the conversation. Use audible 'reflection' to verify that you accurately understand what is being said. Maintain eye contact as one way of indicating that the person speaking has your attention.

Consider this list as a menu from which to choose areas for improvement:

◆ Use appropriate body posture and eye contact.

◆ Use vocal affirmation and nod your head when it is fitting.

◆ Ask questions and probe for understanding.

◆ Ask for more information.

◆ Give feedback by summarizing or repeating the message in your own words.

◆ Empathize with the speaker.

◆ Let the speaker finish before you begin to speak.

◆ Give undivided attention to the speaker and what the speaker is saying.

◆ Observe the speaker's nonverbal messages.

After you have listened, seek clarification and/or deeper understanding. Ask, "Are you saying that...?" Or, "I want to be sure I understand. What did you mean by '_____'?"

> Beware of the temptation to manipulate a conversation into coming back around to your interests.
>
> **warning!**

Once while conducting a capital campaign feasibility interview I encountered a unique opportunity to listen and respond strategically. Roger Crowder was passionate about youth programs, and had been a generous supporter of my client for many years. That generosity dropped sharply three years earlier when the Youth Haven made a decision that he opposed. Nevertheless, Roger was considered to have the potential for a leadership gift to the organization, so off I went to seek his insight on the proposed campaign.

The interview began pleasantly enough, but soon became tense when Roger protested, "I hope you don't have very high expectations of me, because I'll never give them another dime!"

My purpose in conducting the interview wasn't to obtain a gift or pledge. But I did want to assess the likelihood of seeking financial support at a later date. I was there to listen, and this declaration was Roger's clue that he had something more to say on the topic. I could have simply acknowledged the objection and ended the interview. But that just didn't seem like the right thing to do.

Instead, I put down my pen, leaned back in my chair, and asked Roger to tell me more. He said, "I was a big supporter of everything they (the client) did until they made that dumb decision just a few years back. It really offended me and they know it and I just can't support them any longer."

Now, I had been advised about the issue Roger referred to, and I knew the decision would not be reversed. There were too many other personal and material ramifications involved to allow any change to take place. I decided to listen more actively by asking Roger to elaborate. "Why do you feel so keenly about that issue?"

I asked.

He told me.

Roger shared with deep emotion how badly he felt when, as he saw it, his opinion was ignored entirely in favor of someone else's preferences.

I listened.

I paid close attention to what Roger was saying.

I didn't argue, justify, condemn or defend.

I listened actively and compassionately.

From the Donor's Perspective

"The fundraiser is really listening to me! My private thoughts are valuable and I can trust her with my thoughts. I think I can also trust her to carefully use my money."

viewpoint

Roger held nothing back.

After he was finished venting there was an opportunity for me to respond. And since the next chapter is about that very topic, I'll save the rest of the story for later. But for now, suffice it to say that what eventually happened was different than I would have ever expected.

Much different!

To Recap

Plan of Action

◆ Rate your own listening skills on this five-point scale:

1. I do not listen to the speaker; I'm absorbed in my own thoughts.

2. I contribute to the discussion but give no indication of having heard others' comments.

3. I send nonverbal messages, such as eye contact or a head nod, to show that I heard what was being said.

4. I accurately refer to the other speaker's comments in making my own statements.

5. I show by my comments that I understand the meaning and feelings behind others' comments.

◆ Identify two things you could do to improve your listening skills:

1. _____

2. _____

◆ Ask two or three coworkers or close friends to rate your listening skills (using the same scale).

◆ Now ask each person to name one way you could become a better listener.

Person A _____

Person B _____

Person C _____

◆ Compile a list of the improvements suggested in the steps above. Select one area to work on.

_____

◆ Create specific steps, with a timeline, for implementing your listening improvement plan.

Chapter Fourteen

Responding in a Manner that Engages

IN THIS CHAPTER

···→ How to be certain, clear, accurate and kind as you respond

···→ How to respond when you don't know the answer

···→ What if you don't know everything?

Although our primary topic is asking, we must also address the topic of how to respond during cultivation and solicitation calls. After asking targeted questions and carefully listening to our prospects' answers, there will be numerous opportunities to respond. We may be responding to a direct question, a criticism or a request for more information. Whatever the case, we must never offer a reply that cuts off further conversation. Instead, faithfully respond to prospects' questions with certainty, clarity, accuracy and kindness.

When a prospect makes a follow-up inquiry, be certain you really understand the focus of the question. Have you ever witnessed a conversation when someone gave an answer that went on and on, but didn't connect to the question that was asked? How frustrating! How common! Yet, how avoidable! To avoid this, begin your response by assuring that you understand the question. "Are you asking '_____'?" As soon as you are certain of the question, it's time to reply. As you do, keep the focus on the prospect. Zero in on her needs and interests. Simply address the question she is asking.

If you know the answer, give a concise reply without addressing all of the implications behind the issue. Just answer the question. If there are additional (or deeper) questions, trust the prospect to raise them. One thing you don't want to do at this point is to create issues for a particular prospect that aren't currently on the prospect's mind.

When preparing staff and volunteers to make donor calls, I often encounter this apprehension: "What if they ask me a question I can't answer?" I'm amazed how often this question arises. So let me offer this assurance: If you skillfully engage your prospects in thoughtful consideration of a project, there *will* be questions you simply cannot anticipate.

The fact that you have not and cannot anticipate every question is not a shortcoming. The critical issue is what you do when the questions come.

Here is one way to respond when you do not have the answer to a given question. After clarifying what the real question is, I have found it useful to say: "I'm sorry, but I don't have that answer. May I find out and get back with you?" Simple. Straightforward. Direct.

When I reply this way it almost always spawns one of these two reactions:

1. "Yes, I would appreciate that," or,

2. "That's not necessary. I was just curious. It's not really that important to me."

Even with all of my experience, there's really no way to predict which reaction will occur. Regardless of which reaction you receive, follow up anyway. Your prospects will appreciate your diligence and the fact you are attentive to their needs.

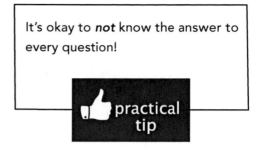

It's okay to *not* know the answer to every question!

practical tip

Another error in this area is attempting to answer a question when you don't know what the answer is. This happens more often than one might expect. Let's look at one way to avoid this pitfall.

First, realize that it's okay to *not* know everything. As mentioned above, people will ask questions you are not prepared to answer. And that's OK. This leads to another reality: It's *not* okay to offer a guess when you *don't* know the answer.

I have had numerous opportunities to observe this behavior firsthand. For many years I met with a board that included a member whose specialty was chasing obscure financial details. In meeting after meeting, when the treasurer presented the financial statements, this board member would ask a question about some monetary minutiae. I knew the treasurer quite well and it was evident to me when he moved from 'knowing' to 'guessing.' This took place often. Unfortunately the treasurer, like most of us, had a real knack for guessing *incorrectly* which would generate follow-up questions and more mistaken 'guesses.' As you might imagine, this rapidly led to a dead end that eventually became embarrassing for the treasurer and greatly frustrating to the board member. It could have easily been avoided by employing the recommendation outlined above.

The most detrimental effect of guessing rather than admitting your uncertainty is that it inevitably undermines your own credibility. That sometimes creates a negative reflection on the organization as well. This scenario can easily be avoided.

I was involved in a cultivation call once when the prospect asked which faculty offices would be relocated within the new academic building that was under construction. Rather than simply answering the question and moving on, the CEO mentioned that some controversy had arisen on campus about this topic. I watched as the prospect literally backed away from his previous enthusiasm to sponsor the office for the department chair. It was clear that he had no interest in getting involved in an ugly 'turf battle.' How unfortunate! The campus controversy regarding office locations was short-lived and was soon only a distant memory for a handful of people. The CEO's response, however, made this a focal point for the prospect, and it eventually became an issue for others with whom the prospective donor spoke.

As we wrap up the topic of Responding, let me finish the story of Roger Crowder. (If you need a refresher, go back to Chapter Thirteen, *The Essential Practice of Listening*.)

Roger had just unburdened his soul regarding a hurt he suffered from an action taken by an organization he had long supported. I knew the decision would not be changed, and I was in no position to act on behalf of the nonprofit organization.

I asked Roger about his strong feelings.

Roger shared his answer.

I listened intently.

I identified sympathetically with Roger by saying, "I can see why you felt so badly. I would have felt the same way."

Then I did something that is difficult for anyone to do. I offered a sincere apology. I said, "I'm so sorry for the way things worked out."

Roger acknowledged my comment by saying, "That's OK; it's not your fault."

This provided an opportunity to shift the discussion from the problem to a solution. So I asked, "Roger, what would have to happen for you to resume your support of this worthy agency?"

After a moment's reflection Roger offered, "If they let me choose the architect for the new building I might give $5,000 toward the project." "Wow!" I thought, "That's a huge increase from his previous offer." I was amazed, but still skeptical.

The rest of the interview was cordial but unremarkable. When it concluded, Roger apologized for "being so candid earlier." I thanked him for trusting me with his openness and replied, "My purpose in being here today was to listen to your thoughts. Your forthrightness allowed me to do my job. Thank you." Then I continued by saying, "I just hope you and Youth Haven will be able to resolve your differences and restore the relationship you once enjoyed." That was the end of my interaction with Roger, but it's not the end of the story.

I had just given Roger a valuable gift.

I didn't take any action on his behalf. To do so was beyond the scope of my involvement in the project.

I didn't solve the problem. The decisions made by Youth Haven had already been finalized.

What I did was listen. And then respond in a way that was fitting. I simply showed that I cared about Roger and how he felt.

Here's what Roger did. A few weeks later, on his own initiative, Roger presented his campaign pledge to Youth Haven's executive director. His pledge was not "a dime." It was not "$5,000." He pledged one million dollars (that's $1 million)!

The significance of his gift goes far beyond the amount. Roger announced that this pledge would outstrip his giving to all other causes for the next three years. Combined!

To me, the most noteworthy aspect of this story is that a relationship was restored. This book opened with an assertion that fundraising effectiveness is more about the relationship than the transaction. My experience with Roger is a resounding affirmation of this principle.

Always remember *it does pay* to listen carefully and respond caringly. *Literally!*

To Recap

Plan of Action

◆ What is your *biggest obstacle* to responding in a manner that engages your audience?

_____

◆ What *change in behavior* do you need to make to overcome this obstacle?

_____

◆ *Who* can come alongside and support you in this change?

_____

◆ *When* will you take the first step?
___/___/___ @ ___:___

Section D—The *People* Involved in Asking

IN THIS SECTION

T his section identifies who should be involved when seeking major donations and outlines the personal qualities they must have in order to enjoy long-term success in fundraising. Executive directors and development directors become very serious about this topic once the decision is made to embark on a major fundraising campaign. These chapters enable fundraisers to build on their existing (but often inadequate) skills, thus increasing their confidence and competence.

We've all probably heard the saying that 'people give to people.' But, while that's true, it really doesn't go deep enough to be meaningful. Stated more fully...

People give to people...
    ...they know and trust...
        ...who give...
            ...and who ask...
                ...for a specific amount...
                    ...for a specific purpose...
                        ...at a specific time.

Let's break this down to its basic components to really grasp the concept.

People give to people they know. Have you ever been asked for a gift by a stranger? Such requests lack the comfort that is automatically present when approached by someone you know.

People give to people they trust. Even though you know the solicitor, if you don't trust them, you're less likely to give.

People give to people who give. Hank Rosso, in his fundraising classic, *Achieving Excellence in Fund Raising,* states what should be obvious, "an asker must a giver be." The leadership principle requires that the solicitor must not ask a prospect to do what they have not already done themselves. Sometimes the prospective donor will ask, "How much did you give?" But even if the question isn't asked outright, human beings seem to have an invisible way of transmitting whether they are personally invested in a project or not. Those of us in fundraising leadership should insist that no one be sent out into the fundraising 'marketplace' without being fully equipped to do their job by—first of all—making their own personal financial contribution.

People give to people who ask. This is an especially important point. Do not assume that the other party already knows what you are after. Make it explicit. At the appropriate time, simply state: "The reason we wanted to see you today is to ask for your consideration of a leadership gift toward the Healthy Hearts campaign." There—you said it. No more guessing is required. Now you just have to proceed with the details of the proposal. (See Section F, *Asking*).

People give to people who ask for a specific amount. At this point I realize that my philosophy differs from many others. Some would suggest that you should 'do your research,' decide what amount is needed to reach the funding goals, and stick with that number until the prospect finally agrees. Instead, I recommend that you use an approach that is far more 'donor focused.' Do your research—yes! But the very best prospect research consists of *speaking with the donor.* Ask her what her vision is for this particular cause...via this charity...for these specific priorities... at this precise time. Each of these variables affects the donor's answer to the question, "How much should I give toward this request." And to state it again, no one can correctly evaluate all of *these* factors apart from the prospect herself. Once we have asked her to do this evaluation, and listened to the result, we are ready to ask about the specific amount. (More in Chapter Twenty-Three, *Asking about Amount.*)

People give to people who ask for a specific purpose. People care differently about the needs that require funding. The person who has an affinity for program staff may have little interest in the new administrative computer system. The one who is passionate about endowment may disdain another construction project. But, once again, we don't determine these interests...we discover them. (See *Asking about Purpose,* Chapter Twenty-One.)

People give to people who ask at a specific time. Making a gift today is an entirely different proposition than agreeing to make a gift over the next three years. In either case, it's important to be specific about the request. If you need one thousand dollars in the next ten minutes, I'm not the right person for you to talk to. But if given enough time, I could come up with that amount of money...and perhaps more.

Understanding the importance of bringing people face-to-face with other people to discuss something as important as a significant gift provides a good backdrop for scheduling a cultivation call.

Bear in mind that we are in an exploratory mode—not an evaluation of the donor and his wishes. Regardless of what the prospect says regarding his intentions, desires and motivations *he is not wrong.* We are not in the business of force fitting people into funding our organization. It *is* our duty to find the point at which the donor's interests, priorities and resources intersect with our agency's plans.

Focus the Ask

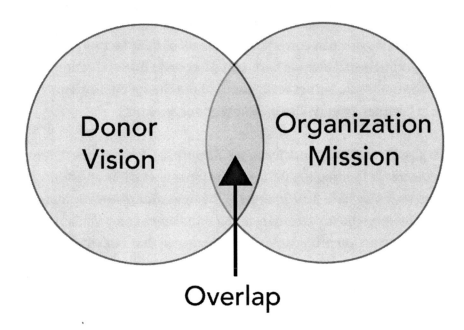

Fundraisers' discussions should always be focused at the point where the donor's vision overlaps with the charity's mission.

Read on to understand the reasons for this combination.

Chapter Fifteen

The CEO as 'Chief Decider'

IN THIS CHAPTER

····→ Delivering on high stakes promises

····→ The assurances of the 'top dog'

There are many people involved in delivering the programs offered by nonprofit organizations. A variety of these individuals could be involved in making gift solicitations. Why do I insist that the chief executive officer (CEO) be a member of the call team when soliciting major gifts? It's just that—this person is the *chief* executive.

As a rule, our prospect will either be the top executive in his organization, or he will be a primary influencer. The gift that is being discussed is a significant amount for the donor. The project (campaign) to be funded will be transformational for the nonprofit organization. And the case for support makes bold claims about the impact a successful campaign will have on meeting critical community needs. A positive gift decision will require serious commitments to be made by both entities. At some point, a corporate CEO (or foundation trustee, or high net wealth individual)

From the Donor's Perspective

"Before I commit to making a large gift, I have to be confident that you can deliver the results you are promising."

will look across the table and ask, "If I contribute the amount you are asking for, can you assure me that the results you described will actually be achieved?"

This is a big question. It deserves a thoughtful response. In fact, a donor's decision to make the gift often hinges on this pivotal aspect of the solicitation. Experience suggests that no one, other than the CEO, can provide a convincing answer. You see, the ability to deliver on such promises is vested in the CEO. And no matter how committed, confident or enthusiastic a program officer, development director, finance manager, counselor or teacher may be, they do not have the authority a CEO does to carry through and deliver such results.

Our draft gift proposal in Chapter Eight indicates that Healthy Hearts Early Childhood Education Center plans to build a new facility and is asking Katie and Jason Rutherford to make a very large naming gift toward the Activity Room. The Rutherfords haven't made a $1.5 million gift before. They are being asked to propel the organization to a new plateau of service with their very large, generous donation. This is all new for Healthy Hearts. There is just one chance to 'get it right.' It's reasonable for the donor to take measures to assure themselves that the person at the top of the nonprofit organization can carry through from concept to completion. The CEO offers assurances (no guarantees). No one else can.

To Recap

Plan of Action

     ◆ Is your *CEO* prepared to be an active member of the call team?
        ❏ Yes
        ❏ No

◆ If the answer is 'No,' what needs to happen to prepare the CEO to fulfill this important responsibility?

_____

◆ *Who* can help make this happen?

_____

◆ *When* will you take the first step?

___/___/___ @ ___:___

Chapter Sixteen

The Volunteer as 'Chief Influencer'

IN THIS CHAPTER

···→ Why involve volunteers?

···→ Why select a peer?

···→ What difference does influence make?

T he second person in the call team is a volunteer who is a peer to the prospect.

First we must address the question, "Why a volunteer?" Previously we outlined the importance of the nonprofit's CEO as an essential member of the call team. The 'Chief Decider' is the top person inside the nonprofit organization who can deliver the results promised by a major fundraising campaign. The volunteer is necessary for a different reason. Key volunteers provide an external validation to the claims and assertions made by the CEO.

Think about this: The CEO (or any other employee) of the charitable organization has an *obligation* to speak favorably on behalf of the agency who issues her paycheck each month. The volunteer, however, is not under any such obligation. So when a volunteer steps forward to vouch for the plans, programs and priorities of an agency, this endorsement conveys a different meaning than when an employee speaks exactly the same words.

The next question to be answered is, "Why a peer?" We have stated repeatedly that fundraising—at its best—is about relationships. Part of the reason for involving a peer is because of the relationship that already exists between the prospect and the peer. It's easier for a gift decision to be made with confidence when one of the askers is already well known by the prospect.

> **People give to people…**
>
> … they know and trust,
>   who give,
>   and who ask
>   for a specific gift
>   for a specific purpose
>   at a specific time.
>
>  practical tip

In Chapter Twenty-Three, *Asking about Amount,* we will prepare fundraisers to assist donors in making an appropriate gift decision in light of the donor's own circumstances. The call team is working to assist the prospect in making a gift decision that will make the giver happy in the immediate…and remain satisfied many years from now. So it only makes sense to engage people in the process who also have a special connection with the potential funder.

The third question to be addressed with respect to the volunteer as 'Chief Influencer' is "What influence?" Everyone has a circle of influence. One's influence can either be used for a constructive purpose or simply wasted. By involving a volunteer in asking peers to make a wise charitable investment, we exercise a positive use of influence. One facet of influence is implied…a silent validation by simply being present. Another aspect of the positive influence must be explicit.

For example, we understand the importance of askers also being givers. And while this qualification can be taken for granted, or assumed, it's important to make it visible— appropriately. Here's how that might be conveyed:

[Peer to the prospect]: "I want you to know that I'm asking you to do something that I have already done myself. This community need is so important to my spouse and me that we have made this project our top charitable interest for the next three years. And, while I'm certainly not suggesting that your pledge should be the same amount as ours, I would challenge you to give at a level that is significant for your own circumstances."

> We want peer solicitors to build on their close personal relationships. But be careful that the connection isn't *too close*. The involvement of a family member or business partner might cause the prospect to feel undue pressure or that their confidentiality is in jeopardy. Each member of the call team must be strategically selected based on the specific dynamics in play with that prospect.
>
> **warning!**

Making such a statement will convey that:

◆ I (the volunteer solicitor) am donating my own money to the project.

◆ My spouse and I are both involved in the decision to contribute.

◆ I think the project is worthy of the generous support of others.

◆ Our gift covers multiple years.

◆ I believe the prospect's circumstances would allow a gift that would be 'significant.'

◆ I'm respectful of the prospect's eventual decision.

With an appropriate call team in place, you are ready to master the other facets of Conversational Fundraising.

To Recap

Plan of Action

◆ *Identify* the ideal peer solicitor for each of your top twelve major gift prospects:

	Prospective Donor	*Peer*
1.	_____	_____
2.	_____	_____
3.	_____	_____
4.	_____	_____
5.	_____	_____
6.	_____	_____
7.	_____	_____
8.	_____	_____
9.	_____	_____
10.	_____	_____
11.	_____	_____
12.	_____	_____

◆ *Invite* each peer to become a member of a call team for approaching the respective donor.

◆ *Equip* the peer for effective cultivation and solicitation.

◆ *Schedule* the first meeting with the prospect.
   __/__/__ @ __:__

Chapter Seventeen

Sincerity, Character & Integrity

IN THIS CHAPTER

···→ The importance of personal qualifications to success in fundraising

···→ How to demonstrate true professionalism

···→ Why transparency matters

Any wholesome principle can be distorted in a way that becomes manipulative, coercive, or misleading. I suppose that is also true for the techniques offered in this book. Certainly that's not what I have in mind. So it seems like a good idea to offer a few words about sincerity, character, and integrity.

The fundraising profession is an honorable one. It involves high trust relationships, and requires a certain degree of diplomacy. In 1993, four national organizations with an interest in the practice of philanthropy joined together and formulated the *Donor Bill of Rights* (see Appendix B). This declaration provides a reliable standard against which to measure fundraising activities. The fundraiser's role—whether professional or volunteer—is to assist prospective donors in making informed decisions about where to invest their charitable dollars. *There simply is no room in our profession for anyone who wants to take advantage of others.* At the end of this chapter you will find a self-assessment that will assist in examining your suitability for this field of work.

According to Roget's 21st Century Thesaurus, *character* is what one is; *reputation* is what one is thought to be by others. As fundraisers, we must measure up on both counts. If your motivation as a fundraiser is not to serve the needs of others, please find a different line of work.

On the other hand, if you are putting your constituents' purposes and vision ahead of your own, let's continue down this path together. World renowned speaker, Zig Ziglar, often admonishes, "You can have everything in life you want, if you will just help other people get what they want."

> **Character**
>
> *You can out-distance that which is running after you, but not what is running inside you.*
>
> —Rwandan Proverb
>
>

In today's world of instantaneous communication it's natural to believe that any message is suitable for email, texting, Twitter, Facebook, etc. Beware of this assumption. These tools are great ways to *maintain* a relationship, but they're no substitute for meeting face-to-face to *establish* a relationship. Research reveals that people are still hungry for genuine friendship. (This is especially true for high net worth individuals.) That's not to suggest you will become golf buddies with the retired corporate executive you are calling on. Or that you will be invited to join the bridge group your prospect belongs to. But you can show a sincere interest in the life and well-being of those whose funds you seek.

True sincerity requires that we notice if there is a mismatch between the donor's priorities and those of our charitable organization. If the right connection doesn't appear to exist, it is the fundraiser's duty to investigate. (See the Association of Fundraising Professionals Code of

Ethical Principles and Standards in Appendix A.)

It may be necessary to express something like this: "I truly appreciate your interest in donating to Healthy Hearts. However, I'm beginning to wonder if your primary interest lies in programs we don't offer. It would be a mistake for us to launch a new program simply to attract your contribution. Could I encourage you to contact ABC Charity? They are the leading provider of XYZ services and could certainly make good use of your gift."

To be *sincere* is to be:

1. free of deceit, hypocrisy, or falseness; earnest;
2. genuine; real;
3. pure; unmixed; unadulterated; or
4. sound; unimpaired.

From Dictionary.com

This situation may require you to say, "Goodbye" to a gift that otherwise looked like a 'sure thing.' If you discover this kind of mismatch and have to step back, it may not feel good at the time. But remember: We agreed to conduct our work on a long-term, donor focused, mission centered basis.

When redirecting a prospective donor as described above, it may seem like a disservice to the organization for which we raise funds. Be assured, however, that if you must disengage with someone, the person whose gift you directed elsewhere will be better served in the process. The prospective donor will tell others about the integrity you demonstrated. Your character, and that of the charitable organization you represent, will be demonstrated with unmistakable

Integrity

Integrity is one of several paths. It distinguishes itself from the others because it is the right path, and the only one upon which you will never get lost.

—M. H. McKee

You can have everything in life you want, if you will just help other people get what they want.

—Zig Ziglar

clarity. Your reputation will be enhanced in ways that money cannot buy. It's "doing the right thing even when you think no one is looking." But someone *always* is.

Think back to a time when you were tempted to compromise something you knew was right. Which course of action did you take? In the long term did it make you feel proud or embarrassed? Reevaluate your work as a fundraiser. Are there adjustments that need to be made in your motives or methods? If so, remember that the pain suffered when doing the right thing is *temporary*. But the hurt resulting from taking the wrong path can be *permanent*.

Perform a periodic 'sincerity check' to assure that your motivations are honorable. Ask yourself the following questions:

◆ "Do I have a sincere interest in the donor as a person?"

◆ "Am I *only* interested in receiving a gift to help me meet this month's quota?"

◆ "Do I demonstrate a genuine concern for the wellbeing of the prospects with whom I visit?"

◆ "Am I simply trying to manipulate donors' views to line up with the 'needs' of our charity in order to get their money so I can move on to the next person?"

◆ "Are my words, attitudes and actions in line with the nonprofit organization's code of ethics?"

To Recap

Plan of Action

◆ Examine yourself by using the 'sincerity checklist' above.

◆ Ask a friend or colleague to prepare an evaluation from their personal vantage point.

◆ Review the results and determine what improvements you would like to make.

◆ Conduct a reevaluation periodically to assess your progress.

Chapter Eighteen

Everyone Follows the Leader

IN THIS CHAPTER

···➔ The single most important success factor

···➔ Deciding who goes first

Leadership matters. This may be the *under*statement of the century! In major campaigns we talk about the importance of the leadership team, leadership gifts, and leadership skills. And it all matters. A lot! Indeed, strong leadership is the *single most important* key to success in a fundraising campaign. Conversely, poor leadership will derail a campaign more quickly than any other factor.

One of the most important lessons I have learned from researching scores of organizations and accumulating years of experience is: *Everyone* follows the leader. I would suggest that each one of us is a leader. Realizing that people will follow wherever you lead

---

Leadership

Leadership is the single most important campaign success factor.

practical tip

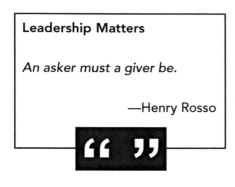

Leadership Matters

An asker must a giver be.

—Henry Rosso

(that's what followers do), the relevant questions are:

1. "*Where* am I leading?" and

2. "*Who* is following?"

The lesson your mother taught you as a child really is true. We *lead* by example. And we *learn* by example. One form of exemplary leadership is summed up in an oft-quoted maxim by Henry Rosso, the godfather of modern fundraising. Rosso succinctly states that, "An asker must a giver be." This is one form of leadership by example. If I give generously to a particular cause and, as a fundraising volunteer, ask others to give as well, I am leading. People will follow. Simply stated, we are not qualified to ask anyone *else* for money until we have made our own gift or pledge.

I have been privileged to work primarily with leaders who are leading to inspiring destinations. But I have worked with others that, by some mystery, think those who follow them will arrive at a different destination than the one to which they are leading.

Some time ago, I provided campaign counsel to a very high profile, well-established, sophisticated higher education institution. When it came to

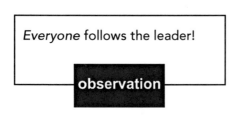

Everyone follows the leader!

observation

making his personal pledge to the campaign, the university president distinguished himself as the most reluctant leader I have ever known. He went to great lengths to conduct research on the giving practices of others in his field. At one point he announced, "Kent, none of my peers have ever been asked to contribute to their institutions." He went on to assert, "I don't see that this is really as important as you say it is." No matter how patiently, kindly, and thoroughly I explained the importance of his pledge, he would not be persuaded.

Eventually, at the insistence of his development director, he turned in a pledge form. It was a three year commitment that totaled less than he would spend on two cups of coffee a day for the same period of time. He could well afford to give many times this amount. And, understandably, he lived in constant fear that others might learn just how much (or little) his gift was.

Oddly enough, he just couldn't understand why his requests for campaign leadership were not met with enthusiasm. He was mystified when others made what he considered to be 'token' gifts to the campaign. Is it any mystery? "How could he *not* understand what was going on?" you may ask. I must confess that I never came up with a suitable explanation either. But this CEO vividly exemplifies the reality that *everyone* follows the leader.

> **Reality Check**
>
> If I give sparingly (or reluctantly, or regretfully) and ask others to contribute, they *will* follow my example.

This leadership principle is especially applicable to fundraising staff and volunteers. The question often arises, "Who goes first?"

"You do!" Who is 'you'? It's whoever is asking the question. The reason is, that's what leaders do—they take the lead.

Sometimes we encounter a situation where no one is asking, "Who goes first?" In this case the nonprofit CEO makes the first pledge. Otherwise the person asking has no basis from which to urge others to act. However, once the leader has taken this step it will be easy to inspire others to do the same.

> **From the Leader's Perspective**
>
> "I will only ask others to do something if I have already done it myself."

As you prepare to demonstrate leadership in this critical realm, ask yourself the following questions:

◆ *Where* am I leading?

◆ *Who* is following?

◆ *Why* do I give?

◆ *Who* do I want to follow my philanthropic example?

◆ Which *barriers* to generous giving can I identify in myself?

◆ How would anyone else (appropriately) know about my generosity/ philanthropy/giving?

> **The Generous Giver says:**
>
> "I want to give *and* leverage the giving of others!"

◆ What is my legacy of generosity *now*?

◆ What will my legacy of generosity be in the *future?*

◆ What would happen if everyone within my circle of influence followed my philanthropic example?

To Recap

Plan of Action

◆ Have I *fully considered* my own level of financial support?

◆ Will the amount of my gift be *inspiring* to others?

◆ *When* will I deliver my gift/pledge?

___/___/___ @ ___:___

◆ *To whom* will I present my gift/pledge?

Evaluate your experience:

◆ *What did you learn* from this particular, personal philanthropic experience?

◆ How did you feel when you presented your gift?

◆ What will you *repeat* in the future?

◆ What will you *do differently* in future gift-giving?

Section E—What to Ask about *Before* Asking

IN THIS SECTION

I n this section we explore topics such as asking about timing, asking about naming, asking about size of gift, asking about form of gift, etc. The unique angle of this section is to provide a specific set of practical tools for readers to put to use immediately—even if reading only this one section.

As mentioned in the introduction, making 'the ask' is generally a big deal. I submit that the 'big deal' can be readily overcome if we will ask the right questions before making 'the ask.' The next eight chapters explain how to ask about the topics that are most critical to the overall decision for philanthropic support.

Since each situation is unique there will be times when one or more of these topics is set aside. Other circumstances will prompt you to *add* questions to your list of what to ask about before making 'the ask.' The main purpose of this book is to equip you to effectively prepare for 'the ask' regardless of the content of the specific request.

Be prepared to adapt the specifics on the following pages to your particular circumstance.

Be creative in how you exercise the practices outlined below.

Don't limit your use of these principles to the topics addressed within these pages.

Be bold.

Have fun.

Make lots of little 'asks' before making 'The *big* ask.'

And be prepared to enjoy the fundraising adventure like you never have before!

Chapter Nineteen

Asking about Meeting

IN THIS CHAPTER

···→ Who should schedule a meeting with prospects?

···→ How should you prepare for the call?

···→ What risks should the caller be alert to?

I n preparing to meet face-to-face with a prospective donor to Ask about Asking, our first task is to set up an appointment. This sounds easy enough, but it can be more complicated than one might expect. There will be numerous meetings to schedule throughout the process. This chapter will help you become more confident as you make arrangements for donor meetings.

Begin by understanding the purpose of the phone call: We are calling to arrange a meeting that will include the prospective donor and the call team (CEO plus the peer volunteer). That's all. One challenge is to avoid the unintended consequences that can occur when scheduling such a meeting.

Before placing the phone call, develop a written plan for the meeting you are calling to schedule. This will ensure that you're knowledgeable and confident about the direction and content of the meeting, so that you will be able to communicate that information clearly to the donor. You will find a sample Contact Plan in Appendix F.

Let's illustrate the concept with a phone call requesting a 'get acquainted' meeting. Jason Rutherford is a high capacity prospect. His friend, Aaron Skinner, is the 'peer' and wishes to introduce Jason to Michelle Gardener, executive director of Healthy Hearts Early Childhood Education Center.

Because fundraising is relationship based, and since Aaron and Jason are friends, the meeting will be scheduled by Aaron. The challenge that can arise when the phone call is placed is for the scheduling call to *become* the meeting. Thus, it will be essential for Aaron to be direct and discreet at the same time.

Prior to dialing Jason's number, Aaron and Michelle must determine the answers to these important questions:

◆ *Who* asks? [Aaron]

◆ *Whom* is Aaron asking? [Jason]

◆ *What* is Aaron asking of Jason? [To schedule a lunch meeting.]

◆ What is the specific purpose for the lunch meeting? [To introduce Jason to Michelle and Healthy Hearts and explore Jason's openness to becoming involved.]

◆ *Why* is Jason being approached? [He is Aaron's friend and a visible leader and generous donor within the community.]

◆ *When* would the lunch meeting take place? [Any Wednesday or Thursday that is convenient for Jason.]

◆ *How much time* will this take? [Ask for 75 minutes, but be prepared to accept less if that is all you can get.]

◆ *Where* will the lunch meeting take place? [California Pizza Kitchen, Jason's favorite hangout, unless another location is more desirable or convenient for Jason.]

◆ *Who* will pay for the meal? [Michelle (Healthy Hearts) will pick up the tab unless Aaron offers to cover it. This should be decided before going to lunch. Jason should not be allowed to buy.]

Also decide what is *not ideal*. For example:

◆ Can't we just do this by phone? [No. This matter is important enough for us to meet face-to-face.]

◆ This sounds like fundraising. Can I just mail you a check instead? [No. There may be a time for us to ask for a gift, but not now. See below.]

Next, understand which parts of the request are *negotiable*:

◆ It doesn't matter *when* we meet. The date and time of day should be at the convenience of the prospect. Get several available dates from the CEO and the peer *before* placing the call.

◆ It doesn't matter *where* we meet. We want the location to be convenient and comfortable for the prospect.

◆ If the meeting involves a meal, ask for 1 hour and 15 minutes, but settle for less if the prospect's schedule dictates otherwise.

◆ It doesn't have to involve food. A mealtime is offered as a convenient way to accommodate the schedule of a busy person.

As you prepare for the phone call, give thought to how you will guide the conversation. It's important to only ask questions for which you are prepared to receive an answer. When asking 'yes' or 'no' questions, be ready to accept either 'yes' or 'no.' On the other hand, if you don't want either 'yes' or 'no,' consider announcing instead of asking.

For example, rather than asking "Do you want to meet for lunch?" consider announcing, "I'd like to get on your lunch schedule. What time would work for you?"

When calling to schedule an appointment, it's essential to be clear and transparent about what you are asking. If you want to meet to ask for a gift, say "I'd like to meet with you to ask for your gift for the upcoming charity ball."

Don't forget the difference between 'asking' and 'announcing.' Be watchful for the perfect time to simply 'announce' the need for a meeting; rather than 'asking' for it—especially if it has already been agreed to.

practical tip

When the meeting is intended to acquaint the prospect with the organization and explore possible interest in future involvement, say "I'm on the board of XYZ Agency and I'd like you to meet our executive director, learn about our work in the community, and explore ways you may wish to be involved."

If they say, "Aren't you just looking for money?" be transparent. "There will be a time to consider financial support later, but right now we would like to bring you up to speed on some big plans we have for the future." The reality is that *we are not ready* to ask for a gift at this time. And *they are not ready* to respond to such a request. *The key is to ask for a gift when both parties are ready to make a fully informed decision about philanthropic support.*

What to say

"I serve on the board of an organization that is doing lots of good work in our state.

I'd like to introduce you to our executive director so you can know more about us and see if you might be open to being involved at an appropriate time.

Could I schedule a lunch appointment for us one day next week?"

practical tip

The possibility of a potential donor saying 'No' to a gift solicitation is not the greatest challenge in fundraising. Rather, the bigger threat occurs when we say 'No' for the prospect. You may ask, "Who does that?" The answer is: You do. I do. Experienced fundraising professionals do. Dedicated board members do. Well-intentioned volunteers do. It's a very common occurrence.

> Ask for the gift *only* when both parties are fully prepared.
>
>  **practical tip**

We don't intend to say 'No' for a gift prospect, but it happens without our even thinking about it. The topic is addressed here to ensure that you *will* think about it. And, having thought carefully about it, you will judiciously *avoid* it.

One way we say 'No' for the prospect is by disqualifying them without making an initial approach. This method surfaces during a brainstorming session to identify potential contributors. One person suggests Katie and Jason Rutherford as possible donors. Someone else in the room asserts, "They won't make a contribution," and goes on to defend the objection. The names are not placed on the prospect list. We just said 'No' for Katie and Jason Rutherford.

> **How we say 'No' for the Donor**
>
> *"He won't give us any money."*
>
> *"She never meets face-to-face."*
>
> *"They don't fund projects like ours."*
>
> *"They've already given."*
>
> **warning!**

Or, someone offers the explanation, "Katie won't meet with anyone face-to-face." Everyone in the room yields and we just said 'No' again.

One of the Rutherfords' acquaintances might say, "They have never funded this kind of project before." We move on to the next name on the list. It's another 'No' for the giver.

And, perhaps the most tragic of all declines—on behalf of another—occurs when someone suggests, "We can't ask them, they've already given (to us or another charity)." The implication is that the donors just gave away their last dollar. That is never the case. Fundraising research tells us that the best source for a gift is someone who has already given. When someone makes a gift they have just self-identified as a donor. Donors give gifts—that's how we identify them. Please refrain from saying 'No' for someone whose behavior is crying out, "Look at me! I'm generous! I like to give! I want to help! I'm a donor!"

> The best source for a gift is someone who has already given.
>
> 👍 practical tip

To Recap

Plan of Action

◆ *Identify the prospective donor* you want to meet with and cultivate a relationship.

_____

◆ Decide *when* you should call to ask for a meeting.
___/___/___ @ ___:___

◆ *Where* is the most appropriate place to hold this meeting?

_____

◆ *Who* will join you when you meet with the prospect?

◆ *What materials* do you need to take along when you meet?

_____

_____

_____

Dr. John C. Maxwell—author, leadership expert, mentor and teacher—explains that "...experience is not the best teacher. If it were, we would all grow from our experiences. *Evaluated* experience is the best teacher. We must discipline ourselves to evaluate what happens in our lives so we can really learn and grow from our experiences." Each of the remaining chapters will end with a section asking you to do just that: *Evaluate* what you just experienced. Discipline yourself and take the time to learn from each contact. Your skills, confidence and comfort level will increase dramatically!

Evaluate your experience:

◆ What was the outcome of the call?

◆ What went well?

◆ What didn't?

◆ How do you feel about the interaction?

◆ What will you *repeat* in future calls?

◆ What will you *avoid* in future calls?

◆ What follow-up is required (next step)?

◆ Who will take the next step?

◆ When?

◆ Later, ask the donor for candid feedback/assessment.

Chapter Twenty

Asking about Giving

T here are countless ways to learn about people...their background, plans and interests. But I enjoy finding out what drives a person's giving habits. One of the best ways to get a glimpse into the hearts of donors is to ask them about their personal charitable development. I call it the 'generosity factor.' Try asking prospective donors one of the following questions:

◆ "How (or when, or where) did you learn to be generous?"

◆ "I notice that you support numerous charities in our community. How do you decide which causes to support, and how much you will give?"

◆ "What do you want your gifts to accomplish?"

◆ "What causes are you so passionate about that you would put your own material resources at risk to address?"

When I have asked people, "How did you learn to be generous?" the answers generally follow these two themes:

◆ "I watched my parents give. That was a significant influence on my giving habits;" or

◆ "I learned to give at church during my childhood."

While these two responses are the most common I have heard, there is no limit to the variety of other experiences that have shaped people's charitable outlook.

I want to share a couple of replies that I will never forget. One came from a retired corporate executive who was raised in a Methodist minister's home. He told me that he "learned to be generous from the tragedy of watching people die rich." How profound! It explained to me why this particular man had such a passion for introducing others to the joy of generous giving. I would never have known this if I had not asked him such a penetrating question. Indeed, I had known him quite well for many years before this conversation occurred and I hadn't a clue!

> **Don't 'hijack' the conversation.**
>
> *Ask* strategically...then *listen* thoughtfully.
>
> **warning!**

The second most memorable reply to the question, "Where did you learn to give?" came from a woman in her early sixties who served on a foundation board. Her reply was, "The thought never really occurred to me until a couple of years ago." I must admit I was startled to realize someone in a position of philanthropic leadership—in a very generous community—had escaped the idea of personal generosity for nearly six decades. This response has provoked me to give serious thought to the ways we perpetuate charitable behavior in our society.

Many years ago Cecil, a retired veterinarian, shared some of his father's sayings with me. In the early part of the Twentieth Century, Cecil's father left Germany to pursue his dreams in the United States of America. This adventurous gentleman, long since deceased, witnessed life from a perspective that is very different from mine. Many of his sayings were memorable, if not profound. One of the quotes that often stirs my mind is, "The tendency of everything is more so." The full impact of that saying didn't hit me immediately. It took some time thinking about it and making observations before I began to grasp its meaning. But I think the old German immigrant had it right. And if "the tendency of everything..." *really is* "...more so," it's sobering. What might this mean for our society? We seem to be more passive in teaching charitable practices than in times past. The old timer's observation doesn't mean that things can't or won't change. But history affirms the idea that it takes great effort to interrupt

---

Perpetuating Philanthropy

Contemporary views about philanthropic education raise some important and challenging questions, especially for those in the baby boom generation. In particular—in light of today's emphasis on confidentiality, anonymity, and electronic transactions—how will our children (or grandchildren) learn about giving from us? Do they see us give? Do they hear our thoughts about generosity? Do we engage them in conversations about when, and where, and how, and how much we give? If not, what are some ways we can creatively engage the next generation in the philanthropic process?

From your own perspective, how effective do you feel we are in carrying out the tradition of philanthropy? Is this being taught within the family structure? Is it happening outside the home? In schools? At church? Elsewhere within the community?

Mull this over and use it as food for thought.

food for thought

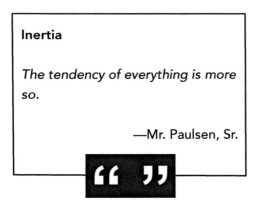

Inertia

The tendency of everything is more so.

—Mr. Paulsen, Sr.

the direction of any culture, society, institution, life or habit. So I offer another question to be pondered by community leaders: How can we instill strong charitable practices into the life and practice of coming generations? More food for thought....

For years, while serving on the faculty of a private college, I met regularly with freshmen students in a mentoring role. One of the courses, called 'Success 101,' included an exercise based on this scenario:

> *The doorbell rings and outside your front door stands Ed McMahon with a big smile on his face, a fussy photographer behind him and an oversized check for $10 million in his hands—with your name on it! He informs you that you have just won the Publisher's Clearing House sweepstakes!*

The assignment required each student to return to class one week later with a written plan explaining exactly what he or she would do with the money. The following introspective questions were asked to help kick-start the process:

◆ What would I begin doing that I am not doing now?

◆ What would I stop doing that I am doing now?

◆ What would I do more of?

◆ What would I do less of?

◆ What would I start?

◆ What would I stop?

◆ Where would I go?

◆ How would I live differently?"

The responses I received seven days later ranged from revealing, to motivating, to disturbing, to inspiring, to shocking, to humbling, to imaginative. Many of these eighteen and nineteen year olds stated specific things they would do philanthropically. A common reply was, "I would begin to give 10 percent of my income to charitable causes."

Out of curiosity, I surveyed the groups, anonymously, to find out how many of them were making systematic gifts out of their present income. Interestingly, approximately 38 percent of them indicated that they already practiced such a discipline. Now, here's the sad reality: Research indicates that, when people experience some kind of windfall, they continue to do what they have already been doing—but just on a larger scale.

"The tendency of everything is more so." Really? *Really.*

Having said all that, here's what I've learned: *Big time generosity starts on a small scale.* If you want to be generous with large sums of money, it's imperative to start with small amounts. Just begin giving.

It may seem strange to write these thoughts in a book

Myth Buster

Misconception: You have to be wealthy to be philanthropic. Or, you must be well-to-do to be generous.

Reality: Philanthropy—voluntary action for the common good—is practiced daily, in numerous ways, by people of very ordinary means. Research reveals this unexpected fact: Americans who earn less than $10,000 per year make up one of the most generous segments of our society! (Measured by contributions as a percentage of taxable income.)

Take away: As philanthropic leaders, we need to be proactive in acknowledging and appreciating the charitable, generous people who surround us.

food for thought

directed to the senior staff of charitable organizations and their board members and other volunteers. Sadly, my experience is that many people who hold these very positions are looking for someone to give *instead of* themselves. My challenge to such individuals is this: Refocus your priorities and begin leading by example. Then look for others who might be inspired to do likewise.

Of course, generosity isn't limited to financial matters. Some people are waiting for their life circumstances to change so they can *begin* to do nice things for others. I would challenge these folks to closely examine their reason for waiting. Any nice gesture that can be done on a large scale can also be done on a small scale. Press yourself to do something out of the ordinary today. Every day!

After exploring the prospect's general attitude about giving, direct the conversation back to the project at hand with this question: "What about Healthy Hearts Early Childhood Education Center? Should we be talking with you about a major gift toward this project?"

This is an important 'permission point'. The prospect's response to this question is critical in determining the direction the conversation will go from here. If the prospect grants permission ("Yes, I would be open to a request for the funding"), we will continue to 'climb *The 10 Step Staircase*' by asking about other aspects of a gift proposal. (See Chapter Six.)

> Thorough exploration *before* making the 'ask' always enhances the solicitation.

practical tip

If permission is *not* granted ("No, I really don't think this is a good fit for my charitable interests"), the discussion will take a different tack. Use the occasion to learn as much about the prospect's reluctance as you can.

To Recap

Plan of Action

◆ *Identify the prospect* you want to ask about giving.

　　_____

◆ Decide *when* you should call to ask for a meeting.
　　__/__/__ @ __:__

◆ *Where* is the most appropriate place to hold this meeting?

　　_____

◆ *Who*, if anyone, will go with you?

　　_____

◆ *What materials* do you need to take to the meeting?

　　_____

　　_____

　　_____

◆ *Prepare* a Contact Plan (Appendix F).

Evaluate your experience:

◆ What was the outcome of the call?

◆ What went well?

◆ What didn't?

◆ How do you feel about the interaction?

◆ What will you *repeat* in future calls?

144 Chapter Twenty ···

◆ What will you *avoid* in future calls?

◆ What follow-up is required (next step)?

◆ Who will take the next step?

◆ When?

◆ Later, ask the donor for candid feedback/assessment.

Chapter Twenty-One

Asking about Purpose

IN THIS CHAPTER

···→ What to ask the prospect

···→ How to keep the conversation donor-focused

···→ Positive and negative purposes for giving

O ne of the challenges enthusiastic fundraisers face is the temptation to overlay their personal passion for the charity on a given donor. People's interests vary. And it's a mistake to assume that every donor will be highly attracted to the same projects as the fundraiser.

We have now climbed to the fourth level on *The 10 Step Staircase*. As you begin *Asking about Purpose* you will share in some very rich conversations. Some people will view this question to be the same as *Asking about Giving*. Others see it as a completely different topic.

Think of these subjects as follows:

Tip for the asker:

Do you feel uncomfortable, uneasy or lack confidence in your asking? If so, admit it openly to the prospect. "I apologize, but I've never really asked someone about their purpose in giving before. I'm feeling a little bit unsure right now...." You'll be amazed at how readily *they* will come to *your* aid.

In *Asking about Giving,* we're asking "What motivates you to give *in general?*" But when we *Ask about Purpose,* the question is "What do you want to accomplish with a *particular* gift?"

The role of the fundraiser (volunteer or professional) is to serve the needs of the donor—not vice versa! Keep in mind, "It's not about me." Therefore, while whatever is happening is not personal to you, it is *very* personal for the donor.

I remember engaging Judy Oliver in such a conversation. I knew she was a well-to-do widow in her eighties. I knew she had a soft spot in her heart for the school. But I was entirely unprepared for her response when I asked what appealed most to her in the overall project.

She explained that she was a retired school teacher. I had no idea! She talked about her passion for educating young children. How she *lived* to expand the horizons of promising—but heretofore undeveloped kids—especially girls. As we visited I discovered that she had been the fifth-grade teacher of one of my employees. Numerous connections emerged.

What to ask:

"What do you want your gift to accomplish?"

I began to understand why she would be deeply interested in funding the school activity room, and why she wasn't drawn toward other aspects of the project.

Judy Oliver's purpose in giving was *entirely* different than what I expected. I'm so glad I asked!

Imagine all I would have missed if I had guessed, assumed, or forged ahead with my own (mistaken) ideas of her priorities!

When you prepare to *Ask about Purpose*, be sure to allow plenty of time. Provide ample opportunity for prospects to talk about their own interest in the project. Ask which aspects of the mission and programs are of greatest interest to them. Explore the reasons behind their answers. How do they see their involvement making a real difference in the community and in the nonprofit organization?

I was contacted recently by a close friend who announced that she and a handful of colleagues were working to establish a shelter for victims of domestic abuse. Acknowledging the substantial amount of work, time and money that would be required to achieve their goals, I asked why she was willing to invest so heavily in a risky start-up venture. "I have seen too many lives shattered by family violence," she explained. "Our research shows that 25 percent of medical emergency calls in this region are caused by some sort of physical or sexual assault by a spouse, partner or acquaintance." She continued by explaining, "This has affected too many people close to me. *I just can't do nothing.*"

Once again, the simple practice of *Asking about Purpose* rendered a crystal clear message about what the donor desired to achieve through her generosity.

After outlining the various projects to be funded by a campaign, ask, "If you had the money to fully fund any one aspect of the project—what would it be?" Be ready to listen...actively. Avoid the desire to share *your* answer. You asked to hear the prospect's thoughts. Listen to them.

What you hear may take you by surprise. It will enlighten you about what the donors hold dear. It will reveal their motivations for supporting the project. It will help you craft a proposal specifically for this one particular individual.

For example, consider the campaign for a new school for hearing impaired children. Because of my personality and background, it's

Perspective

The fundraiser's primary objective is to *serve the donor*.

practical
tip

natural for me to want to fund the classroom for three-year-olds. I can easily envision the teaching and learning that will take place in that room. In my mind's eye I can see activities that will 'turn on the light' to a foundational concept for a precious little girl. I understand the crucial importance of developing specific thinking skills during the fourth year of a little boy's life. I get it. And it seems obvious to me that another generous person would be eager to underwrite a classroom too.

But when I ask someone else for a gift it is *not about me*. We are not the same. They have different interests, priorities, dreams and goals than I do. Their purpose in life is not the same as mine. And, if I try to guess which aspects of the project appeal most to them, I will get it wrong. Almost always! So why not ask someone who really knows? Why not ask the prospects what purposes they want to accomplish with their gifts?

Success

True success is bringing about an informed, appropriate decision.

food for
thought

It is true that some gift decisions are made out of guilt, obligation, pressure, duty or fear. Unfortunately these negative reasons do not produce the kind of gifts that we are looking for: those that are heart-inspired and joyfully made.

The important point is to realize that *ultimately the donor decides* whether to make a gift...or not. And for what purpose. If the decision *really does belong to the donor*, the true measure of success is bringing about an informed decision that is appropriate for his or her circumstances.

Daisy Skaggs and her husband both had long careers in the oil industry. Neither of them held particularly high profile jobs. They had steadily accumulated wealth through wise investing and a modest lifestyle. As an adult, Daisy had enrolled in a foreign language class for her own personal enrichment. Her experience as a student was exceptionally favorable and she began to contribute to the university.

What to ask

"If you had to choose between making a gift toward the new building, the scholarship fund, or our endowment, which would you select? Why?"

When I asked Daisy what she wanted her gifts to accomplish, she offered some valuable insight. "We have no children," she explained. "When I was enrolled at the university I met many students who attend at great cost to themselves and their families. If I can make it possible for even one more deserving young person to get a college education I will feel like I have made a meaningful contribution to the life of someone else's child."

How inspiring! It was my privilege to assure her that the gifts she gave would make a difference for aspiring students. Daisy's purpose in giving was being fulfilled with current giving during her lifetime. Upon her death, the university was notified of a sizable trust that would continue to fund her desired purpose for years to come.

In the final analysis, fundraising is about great ideas and people committed to inspirational causes who join together to create brighter futures for others.

As I was writing the last few chapters of this book, one of my capital campaign clients received the most humbling letter I have ever seen. It expresses another moving purpose for giving. The letter was handwritten from within a medium security state prison and signed by the president of a club formed by a group of inmates. Here is the content in the author's own words:

What to ask

If your prospect has difficulty responding when you *Ask about Purpose*, try one of these alternate questions:

What are you excited about at the moment?

When was the last time you made a difference to somebody?

Who are you really happy for at the moment?

When was the last time you felt inspired?

practical tip

...in keeping with our club's objectives and the mission of the [state] Department of Corrections, we wish to donate our time and resources to those organizations focused on making their communities more effective and safer places to live.

After reading an article in the [newspaper] about your desire and efforts to build a community center...we decided this would be an excellent opportunity for us to show our concern. Enclosed you will find monetary support along with information about our club. We offer this support in good faith, looking forward to hearing from you with information about your goals and objectives and how we might be able to help you accomplish them. *Our club has an earnest desire to deter our youth from making the same mistakes we have and ending up in the same places, confined in prisons and mental institutions, or dead.* [Emphasis added]

If you have any questions you may contact our club sponsor....

Enclosed with the letter was a modest check drawn on the 'Official Depository' of the Department of Corrections. I've never seen such a clear statement of purpose attached to a charitable contribution. You can be sure the amount of the check will be multiplied many times over by its inspiration to other donors and its impact on the many lives that are touched through the new community center.

To Recap

Plan of Action

◆ *Identify the prospective donors* with whom you want to meet to
learn about their purpose for giving:

_____

_____

_____

◆ Decide *when* you will call to ask for a meeting.
___/___/___ @ ___:___

◆ *Where* is the most appropriate place to meet?

_____

◆ *Who* will join you when you meet with the prospect?

◆ *What materials* do you need to take along?

_____

_____

_____

Evaluate your experience:

◆ What was the outcome of the call?

◆ What went well?

◆ What didn't?

◆ How do you feel about the interaction?

- What will you *repeat* in future calls?

- What will you *avoid* in future calls?

- What follow-up is required (next step)?

- Who will take the next step?

- When?

- Later, ask the donor for candid feedback/assessment.

Chapter Twenty-Two

Asking about Form

IN THIS CHAPTER

···➔ Types of gifts

···➔ How investments assist in reaching charitable goals

···➔ How fundraisers develop donors

I n the United States of America, only 9 percent of the wealth is held in cash—the remaining 91 percent is in some other form. That's an interesting statistic, but what does that mean for a fundraiser? It means that if we're looking for and thinking about cash *only*, we may be missing out on the largest potential gifts.

Success in a major fundraising campaign is dependent on securing a fairly small number of rather large gifts. These gifts usually represent the donors' *accumulated* assets, rather than gifts from current income. So be sure to look beyond gifts of cash. Cash gifts often are indicative of a gift of *income*.

To help get prospects to think about non-cash gifts, I like to use the following list as an exploration tool:

TYPES OF GIFTS

- ☐ Cash
- ☐ Stock or other securities (appreciated)
- ☐ Real estate – homes, farms, etc.
- ☐ Mutual funds
- ☐ Donor Advised Funds
- ☐ IRAs (avoid enormous tax liabilities)
- ☐ Trusts
- ☐ Gifts-in-kind – inventory, equipment, vehicles
- ☐ Bequests
- ☐ Insurance
- ☐ Mineral Rights
- ☐ Royalties
- ☐ Intellectual property – software
- ☐ Life estates
- ☐ Charitable gift annuities
- ☐ Community Foundation funds

I'll show the list to a gift prospect and ask, "Which of these methods of giving have you used?" or, "What is your favorite form of giving?"

Listen...

Listen more...

As you listen and gently probe, serious learning can take place. You will discover how well informed the gift prospect is (or isn't) about alternative forms of giving. Your prospect will begin to understand other options for making gifts. And, hopefully, they'll start to think in new ways.

Sometimes I'll ask, in follow-up, "Have you ever seriously considered any of the other types of gifts?" If so, "What caused you to make your gift with cash instead?" Or, "Which options would you be interested in knowing more about?"

You don't have to be a planned giving expert to have this discussion. That's not the point. Simply explore the many ways gifts *can* be made and be ready to assist if the prospect demonstrates a real interest.

> **How we say "no" for the donor**
>
> "She doesn't have any liquid assets."
>
> Or "she *only* has liquid assets."
>
> Or "he won't part with any of his property."
>
> **warning!**

For example, if a donor asks me to explain a charitable remainder unitrust I would have to promptly disclose my ignorance on the topic, "I can't tell you the ins and outs of a CRUT, but I would be happy to introduce you to someone who can. I've been told that this instrument offers ways to maximize your giving, minimize income taxes, and provide a degree of flexibility in your financial situation. Is this something you'd be interested in?" I don't need to be an expert in planned giving, but I do need to know someone who is.

> **What to Ask**
>
> Do you have any property that you don't feel obligated to keep long term?
>
>  practical tip

Another question you might ask is, "Have you ever thought about how your investments might assist you in reaching your charitable goals?" Asking along these lines will often prompt the donor to identify potential gift avenues that she has never considered previously. I have found people to be far more intentional about how to *accumulate* wealth than how to efficiently *dispose* of their investments.

Once I worked with an elderly couple who owned an oil company worth several million dollars. Dennis Clark was a sturdy, stubborn, self-made millionaire who had worked hard all his life. He was now in his eighties— still actively working every day, and losing his hearing. Martha was a traditional homemaker, happy to let her husband handle all financial matters. She was an octogenarian as well, was becoming rather frail and was losing her eyesight. They had one son, now deceased, and had already provided financially for their family to the extent they felt obligated.

Dennis and Martha had numerous reasons why they might have supported the cause I represented. But they were stuck. They had nothing to create a sense of urgency in their gift decision. And, I can assure you, no one was going to push Dennis on the matter.

In discussing the topic with Dennis' financial advisor (Earl) I uncovered two vital—and disheartening—insights into Dennis. First, Earl told me "I've been after him for years to put a will in place, but he 'doesn't have time.' He's too busy making money to plan his estate." Second, Earl informed me that Dennis was negotiating the sale of his oil company. When I asked if Dennis was considering any gifting methods that would maximize his income and reduce the tax burden, Earl said, "Dennis' philosophy is this: 'If I owe Uncle Sam the tax, I just want to pay it.'"

The sad part of this story is that Dennis did sell the business he built over decades of hard work. He received several million dollars in exchange. And, when it was all said and done, the government ended up with more money than Dennis did. And charity got none.

This picture could have looked *so* much different! I wish someone could have encountered the Clarks much earlier and prepared them to make wise, generous decisions at this critical juncture. Think of the *joy* they could have had by giving literally millions of dollars to their alma mater, church, and/or local charities! Think of their *satisfaction* in keeping more of their wealth to use for their priorities, even after "...paying Uncle Sam everything I owe him."

And most unfortunate of all, in just a few short years they both died...still without getting around to writing a will. *Sad.*

My point in sharing this story is this: As fundraisers, a big part of our work is donor development. We work to assist others in achieving their goals... serving their priorities, whether it benefits our own organization or not. Sometimes our cause isn't the right fit for a particular prospect. But if we don't ask the right questions... don't listen strategically... don't take the time to listen to their heart's desire we can miss golden opportunities of service. When we thoughtfully *Ask about Form* we will likely hear messages that deserve our full attention.

> **From the Donor's Perspective**
>
> "I have assets other than cash that could be easier for me to part with than cash."
>
> **viewpoint**

On a brighter note, I received a phone call one day from Royce, a friend of mine who had moved to another state. He and his wife owned a rental house near the university campus where I worked. Their tenant had recently moved out, and what had been a steady source of income for them had turned into a headache.

Royce indicated that, since he and Helen were semi-retired, they no longer had the energy or interest to keep up with rental property. So he called to ask if I might help him find a buyer for the house.

As I listened, I began to see that the solution he was pursuing didn't really fit the problem he was trying to solve. Not wanting to make a recommendation that might be unwelcome, I asked, "Royce, would you ever consider disposing of your property in a way that might provide an income stream for you and Helen for life?" He replied, "I'm very interested. Tell me more." In response, I gave him a layman's description of a charitable gift annuity and explained that it might be funded with the donation of his rental house.

Rather than bore you with all of the detailed arrangements or technical aspects of the gift, let me fast forward several weeks. Royce and Helen sat across the desk in my office. They had just signed the papers to transfer their house to the university in exchange for a lifetime income. These humble stewards, of modest means, were overwhelmed with gratitude at what I had assisted them with:

1. They no longer had to maintain an aging residential property.

2. They no longer had to collect rent each month.

3. They no longer had to find another tenant to rent the house.

4. They gained a current charitable deduction as part of the gift annuity agreement.

5. They gained a source of income that would continue for their lifetime.

Helen just couldn't contain herself. In unrestrained enthusiasm she exclaimed, "We never dreamed that we'd be able to make a gift of this magnitude! Thank you for making this possible."

Tears of joy coursed down all our faces as we celebrated their generosity. And I was totally unprepared for what happened next.

But that part of the story doesn't fit here. When you read Chapter Thirty-One, *Asking about Recognition*, you'll understand why I'll never forget their charitable example.

To Recap

Plan of Action

      ◆ Identify someone you can ask about different types of gifts.

◆ Decide *when* you should call to ask for a meeting.
___/___/___ @ ___:___

◆ *Where* is the most appropriate place to hold this meeting?

_____

◆ *Who* will join you when you meet with the prospect?

_____

◆ *What materials* do you need to take along?

_____

_____

_____

◆ *What obstacles* stand in the way of completing this assignment?

_____

_____

_____

◆ How will you *overcome* each obstacle?

_____

_____

_____

Evaluate your experience:

◆ What was the outcome of the call?

◆ What went well?

◆ What didn't?

◆ How do you feel about the interaction?

◆ What will you *repeat* in future calls?

◆ What will you *avoid* in future calls?

◆ What follow-up is required (next step)?

◆ Who will take the next step?

◆ When?

◆ Later, ask the donor for candid feedback/assessment.

Chapter Twenty-Three

Asking about Amount

IN THIS CHAPTER

···➔ The most private conversation

···➔ Understanding 'why' before asking 'how much'

···➔ A caution about gift presumptions

···➔ Using the Gift Chart to discuss the range of giving

S hould fundraisers determine the amount for a gift request or should we invite the donor to decide her own level of support? Realizing there is a bit of controversy on the topic, I'm going to state my position (as if there's any mystery about it at this point in the book!) and offer some supporting thoughts.

When it comes to requesting charitable support, fundraisers are not the deciders. The donor decides. An asker may inspire, suggest, request, hope —even beg and plead. But, ultimately the donor makes the decision. Since the donors know all the facts and circumstances behind their decisions, and the fundraiser knows only a few—at most—why not *ask?*

By all means do your donor research. But *please*...don't allow financial data and third party opinions to become a substitute for the donor's 'real time' preferences and priorities. The former approach is quicker, requires fewer 'people skills' and less patience than the latter. The more deliberate approach, however, will pay much bigger dividends over the long run and become a real asset when it comes to word-of-mouth recommendations from donors to their peers.

Discussing the amount of a pledge with a prospective donor can cause even the most experienced fundraiser to break out in an ice cold sweat. This is because we are about to broach a subject that is deeply personal. People tend to be *very private* about *their* money matters. And that's a key point: it's *their* money.

Another suggestion I like to have made by a solicitor is how much it is hoped I will give. Of course such a suggestion can be made in a way that might be most annoying. I do not like to have anyone tell me when it is my duty to give. There is just one man who is going to decide that question—who has the responsibility of deciding it—and that is myself. But I do like a man to say to me, 'We are trying to raise $4 million, and are hoping you may be desirous of giving blank dollars. If you see your way clear to do so, it will be an enormous help and encouragement. You may have it in mind to give more; if so, we shall be glad. On the other hand, you may feel you cannot give as much, in view of other responsibilities. If that is the case, we shall understand. Whatever you give after thinking the matter over carefully in the light of the need, your other obligations and your desire to do your full share as a citizen, will be gratefully received and deeply appreciated.' When you talk to a man like that, he is glad to meet you again, and will not take the other elevator when he sees you in the corridor because you backed him to the wall and forced him to give.

— John D. Rockefeller, Jr.

" "

It's easy to talk in the abstract about the importance of a fundraising project, but when it comes to the amount of *my* contribution it really gets personal. Since this is such a personal matter, it must be addressed in a very personal way. Consequently, we proceed to this topic with a healthy dose of respect (if not apprehension!).

Sequence Matters

Ask 'why' *before* asking 'how much.'

practical tip

Deciding on the amount of a gift is not a simple consideration; it is complex. This underscores the importance of *Asking about Amount* only *after* addressing the other elements of the gift context. In previous meetings with the donors we discussed the compelling case for our fundraising campaign. We quantified the social and financial costs of acting later rather than now. We demonstrated the impact their investment will have on the lives of those we serve. Now that the donors have embraced the purpose behind the fundraising campaign, it's time to engage them in a conversation about the amount they might contribute.

How we guess for the donor

When we substitute our 'research' for the donor's personal input we end up asking for an 'arbitrary' amount based on what they have given other (seemingly similar) causes. This amount may be significantly higher—or lower—than their potential support for this project.

warning!

As you prepare for *Asking about Amount* with a specific funder, it is wise to go back and review the *Two Risks to Avoid* in Chapter Nine. You will want to ask your questions and guide the conversation in such a way that you do not invite a premature response, regardless of whether it is a 'yes' or 'no' that comes too early.

My 'Big 3'

Effective fundraising is all about:

1. Relationships (not transactions)

2. *Organizational mission (not individual needs and desires)*

3. *Long-term objectives (not today's crises and pressures)*

food for thought

The panic question that often surfaces is 'What if they give less than we need from them?' 'What if?' Indeed! This is a very real scenario *regardless* of how the prospect is approached. My position on this issue is just another expression of my *'Big 3'* philosophy. There will be many occasions when the amount of the gift will be different (more or less) than the nonprofit organization might have envisioned. But there is a priority that is far more important than the size of this particular gift commitment. We always want to treat others in a way that:

◆ honors and preserves the relationship;

◆ supports the valuable mission of the nonprofit organization; and

◆ positions the nonprofit organization to make other successful asks for future gifts.

It really goes back to a fear of the unknown. We all have a tendency to anticipate the most negative scenario when someone else is 'steering the ship' (driving the conversation, etc.) This is one reason to begin a cultivation call with an introduction that goes something like this:

Don't be presumptuous about the gift decision someone might make. It is *so easy* to 'step out of bounds' on this topic. This is a perfect place to *ask* for permission. Such as, "Katie and Jason, you've explained why children's art programs are so close to your hearts. Would I be out of line to ask what range of gift we should be talking about?"

warning!

Monica [peer]: "Katie, Jason, I'm so glad we were able to get together today with Michelle [CEO]. This project is so important to the children in our community. But I want to put you at ease. We're not here to ask you to make a gift today. There will be a time for that, but it's not now. What we'd like to do today is discuss specific ways you might be involved. But first, I'd like Michelle to tell you about something that happened just last week at the Education Center."

> **From the Donor's Perspective**
>
> "Please don't make me guess about the real need. Put everything 'on the table' and let me make an intelligent, informed decision."
>
> **viewpoint**

Notice the phrase "...specific ways you might be involved." It's intentionally vague. It implies the donors *would* like to be involved. (Remember, we asked earlier, "Could you ever see yourself being involved in a project like this?" They said "Yes." We now have an *obligation* to help them fulfill their desire to help solve a community problem.) It gives the prospect room to define their personal involvement in a way that suits their own needs and desires.

Previously, when we *Asked about Giving*, we listened as the prospects described how they felt when they made their *largest* gift ever.

When we *Asked about Purpose,* the donors talked about what they would like to accomplish with their gift.

In *Asking about Form* we focused on gifts of every type *except* cash...lifting the prospects' sights even further.

> **How we say 'No' for the donor**
>
> 'We can't ask them...they wouldn't (or couldn't) give at that level!'
>
> **warning!**

The peer and executive director (call team) should be prepared to speak briefly about their own personal commitments and the

The Principle of Proportional Giving

Donors who make large gifts often know where they want their support to fall in relation to the amounts that will be given by others. Don't confuse them by being vague about the total amount needed and the numbers and size of gifts required to reach your goal. Share the gift chart frequently.

practical tip

gift or pledge that each of them has already made. Then they can encourage the prospect to 'join us in making a generous (or sacrificial) contribution.' This is an important leadership moment. (You might want to revisit Chapter Eighteen, *Everyone Follows the Leader.*)

It is time now to take step #6 on *The 10 Step Staircase*. Keep the purpose of the meeting clearly in mind. We are not here today to ask for a gift. We are obtaining the prospect's input so we can prepare a personalized gift proposal.

Our discussion about the amount of the gift is set within the context of the fundraising goal. The 'No Boundaries' capital campaign underway for Healthy Hearts Early Childhood Education Center has a goal of $10 million and is built on the sample gift chart illustrated on the next page.

It's natural now, when introducing the gift chart, for us to focus on two specific places on the page: the bottom line and the top line. The bottom line reiterates the overall campaign goal we have been discussing. And the top line indicates the amount of the largest gift required to reach that goal. This provides *context* for the discussion.

A carefully crafted gift chart will enable the prospect to see where he fits in with others who will fund the project.

practical tip

Now it's time to *Ask about Amount*. With the gift chart in front of the donor, let me suggest that you inquire along these lines:

"When it's time to make your own contribution to this project, where could you see yourself on the gift chart?"

"As you think about what you would like to accomplish over the next three years, what *range of gift* should we be talking about?"

When *Asking about the Amount,* use the term 'range of gift'. One reason for this is to make it easier for the prospect to respond. When we're asked

Sample Gift Chart*

Leadership Gifts

1 gift of	$1,500,000 for a total of	$ 1,500,000
1 gift of	$1,000,000 for a total of	$ 1,000,000
3 gifts of	$ 500,000 for a total of	$ 1,500,000
<u>6</u> gifts of	$ 250,000 for a total of	<u>$ 1,500,000</u>
11 gifts	totaling	$ 5,500,000

Major Gifts

12 gifts of	$ 100,000 for a total of	$ 1,200,000
18 gifts of	$ 50,000 for a total of	$ 900,000
<u>36</u> gifts of	$ 25,000 for a total of	<u>$ 900,000</u>
66 gifts	totaling	$ 3,000,000

General Gifts

72 gifts of	$ 10,000 for a total of	$ 720,000
84 gifts of	$ 5,000 for a total of	$ 420,000
106 gifts of	$ 2,500 for a total of	$ 265,000
<u>106</u> gifts of	<$ 2,500 for a total of	<u>$ 95,000</u>
<u>368</u> gifts	totaling	<u>$ 1,500,000</u>
445 Gifts	Totaling	$10,000,000

* Notice that the Leadership and Major gifts categories constitute 17% of the donors, who contribute 85% of the dollars. Conversely, the General gifts category comprises 83% of the donors who give 15% of the dollars.

for a specific amount it seems like we're being asked to make a *decision*. But when asked for a range, it seems like a *discussion*.

Another benefit of talking in terms of 'gift range' is that it continues to 'lift the sights' of the donor. For example, if the response is, "Our gift will most likely not be in the leadership gift category," then the discussion will focus on the top of the major gifts level (see the sample gift chart). Consider responding as follows: "That would be a huge boost to the campaign - thank you! The three year pledge you've described could be in the range of $100,000. Now I have a really important question for you. What would have to happen for you to give at that level?"

Question to remember

"What range of gift should we be talking about?"

When approached this way, donors will feel free to engage in a discussion about amount without feeling like they are expected to make an immediate gift decision.

practical tip

After the prospect has indicated the gift range, ask, "How will you decide between $_____ (high amount) and $_____ (low amount)?"

The follow-up conversation might flow like this:

[Solicitor] "What *range of gift* should we be talking about?"

[Prospect] "Our gift will probably be between $500,000 and $750,000."

[Solicitor] "Wow; that is really generous! How will you decide between $750,000 and $500,000?"

[Prospect] "It will depend on how the stock market treats us in the next three months."

-or-

[Solicitor] "What would need to happen for you to make your gift at the higher level?"

[Prospect] "It will depend on whether I am approved to become a partner in the law firm."

The way we respond to the donor's answer to our question about gift range will either validate our sincerity and professionalism, or reveal our pretense. If we hear an indication of a modest gift, abruptly pick up our materials and head for the door, we are telling the prospect that it really *is* all about the money. However, if we continue to be genuinely interested, caring and patient, it reinforces the idea that every gift matters.

> **Key Question**
>
> Ask the prospect, "If you were *fully informed* and *adequately motivated*, what would have to happen for you to give at the higher level?"

Once while I was conducting a feasibility study I interviewed someone who had a very unpleasant experience during a previous feasibility interview. She recalled, "As soon as he [the interviewer] realized that mine would be a modest gift, he closed his notebook and couldn't get out of the door quickly enough. The whole experience left me feeling exploited. It was a real turn-off!"

As she talked, I heard a sense of betrayal in her voice and saw disappointment in her eyes. You can only imagine the negative effect this experience had on her future relationship with that particular charity.

We convey the same professionalism – or shallowness with an ill-advised response to a *positive* answer. You simply must be genuine and professional in every situation. Period.

When discussing the size of a gift, an evaluation of the amount begins immediately. Regardless of whether the topic is voiced openly or not, everyone present engages in this process. As soon as a specific amount is mentioned, we begin to think 'That's a lot of money' (or 'That's not very much money'). The magnitude of a gift amount is measured relative to the size of other gifts. So we have to get comfortable with the concept of 'compared to what'? There may even be times when we will actually *voice* this question. But for now, let's look at some likely points of comparison for a gift amount.

'That's a lot of money' *compared to:*

- ◆ what's in my wallet right now,

- ◆ my next paycheck,

- ◆ the other gifts I ordinarily make,

- ◆ my monthly or annual salary,

- ◆ my bank account,

- ◆ my investment portfolio,

- ◆ my net worth,

- ◆ the overall cost of the capital project, or

- ◆ the community problem we seek to solve.

The points of comparison could be limitless, but the lesson is the same: Discussion of any particular dollar amount must be done in context. The two most important dimensions of this context are the scale of the overall campaign (thus the use of the gift chart) and the donor's personal resources (financial capacity).

Notice that the first seven measures in this list of nine are comparisons of the donor's financial circumstances. And, even though there are some very sophisticated tools available for donor research, the information provided by those sources is, at best, an educated guess. Since we agreed earlier that 'we won't guess when we can ask,' this is a good place to renew our resolve to *ask*.

But ask what—specifically?

We're not going to ask, "How much money do you have in your wallet right now?" or, "Could you please tell me your net worth today?" First of all, polite people don't make such brazen requests. Secondly, the prospect may not even know the precise answer. And, taken on its own, their exact answer isn't entirely relevant! I suspect we have all made gifts that were greater (or less) than the amount of money we had in our pockets, our checking accounts or our monthly incomes. These three measures point to only one dimension of a gift comparison...liquid resources accessible *today*. There are three other elements that are critical to the equation. They are:

◆ total resources available during the pledge period (this year... three years...five years, etc.);

◆ the magnitude of the social need we are addressing; and

◆ the donor's level of motivation (passion) to become part of the solution.

In my experience, the most important factor in the gift decision is the last: Personal passion for the project. The other factors are not *un*important, but they are *less* important.

It is important for the 'amount' discussion to revolve around the donor's sense of where they fit. And we want to delicately encourage them to maximize their gift.

When contemplating a major fundraising campaign, give strong consideration to a campaign planning (feasibility) study. An independent consultant will conduct personal, confidential interviews with a number of the potential funders. Several topics will be covered, one of which is the question about possible gift size. This process, when carefully conducted, can jump-start the cultivation and solicitation process. For an in-depth discussion of this topic, refer to *Conducting a Successful Capital Campaign* by Kent Dove.

practical tip

To Recap

Plan of Action

◆ *Name the prospective donor* who is ready to be asked about the amount of their next gift or pledge.

_____

◆ Decide *when* you should call to ask for a meeting.
___/___/___ @ ___:___

◆ *Where* is the most appropriate place to hold this meeting?

_____

◆ *Who* will join you when you meet with the prospect?

◆ *What materials* do you need to take along when you meet?

_____

_____

_____

Evaluate your experience:

◆ What was the outcome of the call?

◆ What went well?

◆ What didn't?

◆ How do you feel about the interaction?

◆ What will you repeat in future calls?

◆ What will you avoid in future calls?

◆ What follow-up is required (next step)?

◆ Who will take the next step?

◆ When?

◆ Later, ask the donor for candid feedback/assessment.

Chapter Twenty-Four

Asking about Timing

IN THIS CHAPTER

···→ Two important dimensions of timing in fundraising

···→ Whose timing matters most?

···→ The opinions that really count

There are at least two aspects of timing for us to inquire about: The first is the timing of the gift decision. The second regards the timing of the gift fulfillment. These two factors may be interrelated, but are usually determined by separate and distinct considerations.

As mentioned earlier, these matters are personal in nature so it's helpful to remember that, at this level, timing is primarily about the donor's timeframe...not the organization's. This is not to suggest that the nonprofit organization's timelines are irrelevant, rather that they are generally less important to the donor.

When it comes to urgency in decision-making, I'm reminded of an experience I had as a teen. It was a Monday night in the fall of 1970 and I was making plans for a date on Friday night with a girl from a town twenty miles away. I had a car of my own, a 1951 Chevy sedan, but for some reason I thought it would be more impressive if I were to arrive in my parents' 1968 Buick Wildcat.

I rarely asked to borrow my parents' car...I rarely had reason to...so I was a bit apprehensive about 'making the ask.' What if things didn't go right and my Dad said 'No'?

There I sat in our darkened living room. As my Dad watched Monday Night Football, I waited for just the right time to make my extravagant request. Not wanting to compete with two NFL teams for my Dad's attention, I waited for a commercial break before asking, "Dad, can I borrow your car Friday night?"

Before he gave an answer, the game was back on so I waited. And waited... for what seemed like hours (but was actually just a handful of minutes) while he watched the game.

So, eventually I pressed him again by asking, "How about it? Can I use the car?" And his reply taught me a valuable lesson that I'm sharing with you. He asked me, "How soon do you need an answer? If you have to know right now, I know what the answer will be."

Those two sentences really brought me up short. Suddenly, I realized that there were decision factors at play that went far beyond my self-centered mind. And, in that moment, I discovered that, in order to get a 'yes' answer, I had all the time necessary to wait for his decision. (By the way, he let me borrow the car!)

Whose Timing?

If your fundraising request must be decided based solely upon your own pressures and priorities, be ready to be turned down repeatedly. Alternatively, if you can adjust to the prospect's situation, allowing him the time he needs to come to the decision that is exactly right for his own circumstances, you will be richly rewarded for your patience.

So *you* decide. Whose timing matters most? With this lesson in mind (indelibly, for me), I have found it useful to ask, "When do you feel you could make a decision on something as important as your involvement in this project?" As you listen to the donor's response, you will begin to understand the donor's world and how he approaches matters of importance.

I remember having a similar conversation one January with John, a very busy corporate executive. He had agreed to chair the capital campaign I was involved with and it was time to solicit his gift before approaching other members of the campaign cabinet. I laid out the scenario by saying, "Before we can ask others to contribute to the campaign we must have personal financial commitments from 100 percent of those who are closest to the organization. We have already received pledges from all of the board members, and now it's time to do the same with the campaign cabinet. It's important that you make your own pledge before the others are approached. When would be a good time for you to make your gift commitment?"

John's response was not what I expected. It was not what I hoped for. It was not what I wanted. But his response was what I asked for. And it eventually proved to be better than what I had expected, hoped for and wanted. John said, "I'll have to talk to my tax guy first." "Okay," I thought, "When might this happen?" He went on to say, "I can't make my pledge until my tax return is filed."

At this point, I was faced with a dilemma. By rough calculation there were about ninety days between that mid-January morning and April 15, the due date for his annual tax filing. And that's assuming no extensions! Thus, I realized I still didn't have a very clear idea about when he might make his pledge. So I asked.

Remember, we're *Asking about Asking*. I could have guessed that he would finalize his Form 1040 the first week of February, or perhaps that he would wait until the middle of April. I could have guessed...but my odds of guessing correctly are almost nil. So I asked, "When do you think that might be?"

As we visited further, John described his personal situation in a way that made clear the path forward; a path that made sense for both John and the charity.

From the Donor's Perspective

"I want to give but have to wait until...(the stock market goes back up, these financial instruments mature, next year etc.)."

Think about what John communicated when he said "I'll have to talk to my tax guy first." The amount of his pledge was important enough to him that he wanted to base it on the best information possible. John was looking at the big picture... for him. And just like I promised earlier, we were richly rewarded for being patient. John's pledge, after completing his tax return, was quite generous. And even more importantly, it was *his* decision, made in *his* time and it brought *him* great pleasure as *he* determined the amount of *his* gift. It was a real win-win situation.

Shortly after a rather precipitous time of stock market declines, I met with a generous donor who explained his situation this way: "Fortunately my financial advisor recommended that I divest my stock holdings before the big drop in the market. I'm so thankful for his insight. And I'm glad I followed his advice, minimizing my losses. But my regret is this: I wish I had given those stocks away before they lost their value."

Another lesson I learned regarding timing came very early in a capital campaign. The Griffin Foundation had been generous in supporting the charitable organization for several years. When the CEO made the gift solicitation, it was an impulsive ask for $1 million over three years.

There was nothing about this foundation's giving history that would support such an amount. I cringed. I 'knew' they would come back with a much smaller amount.

I will never forget the phone call I received from Jack Childers, the foundation board president, a few weeks later. He said, "Kent, our board met last night and we approved your request. But we can't do it over three years. If we can have five years, we'll give you $200,000 a year - and make it a million dollars that way. Is that OK?" In my shock I muttered some forgettable words of agreement while Jack continued, "I'm leaving town for a few weeks tomorrow morning. I'll send you a letter with a check for $200,000 before I leave. I need you to sign the letter and return it before you deposit the check. Congratulations!"

That was an abrupt end to a brusque conversation, but it wasn't the end of the story. Due to a large challenge grant from another foundation, there was a big push to reach the overall campaign goal by a certain date. The Griffin Foundation stepped up and extended their pledge for another year, making a total of $1.2 million over six years! This became the largest foundation gift to that campaign. It was record-setting for the donee in other ways as well.

How we say "no" for donors

"They won't give to us because...

◆ ...their money is tied up in real estate."

◆ ...they have 2 children in college."

◆ ...this is a bad year for their business."

◆ ...they just made a big pledge to their church."

watch out!

Strategies for dealing with objections

We can accommodate your time frame.

practical tip

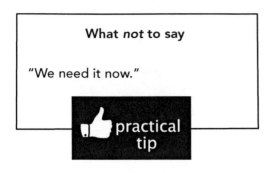

What *not* to say

"We need it now."

Here is the important lesson: I was right in my belief that the Foundation would not give $1 million over three years. But I was wrong in believing they wouldn't give $1 million. I was thrilled to be wrong. I would never have seen my way clear to ask for $1.2 million, but they exceeded my expectations. Dramatically! The timing they chose was just right for them. And, I assure you, there was no objection on the recipient's part to the (eventual) six year gift period they used.

Just to restate, when it comes to the individual donor, the donor's opinion counts. Ours doesn't.

To Recap

Plan of Action

◆ *Whose timeline* do you need to understand?

_____

◆ *When* should you call to ask for a meeting?
___/___/___ @ ___:___

◆ *What will you ask* (exactly)?

_____

Evaluate your experience:

◆ What was the outcome of the call?

◆ What went well?

◆ What didn't?

◆ How do you feel about the interaction?

◆ What will you repeat in future calls?

◆ What will you avoid in future calls?

◆ What follow-up is required (next step)?

◆ Who will take the next step?

◆ When?

◆ Later, ask the donor for candid feedback/assessment.

Chapter Twenty-Five

Asking about Naming

IN THIS CHAPTER

···➤ Discerning who is interested in naming opportunities

···➤ Why use a gift naming brochure?

···➤ "What do these twelve stones mean?"

W e've probably all heard the saying 'There is nothing as important to a person as their own name.' And this reality brings us to the topic of honorary or memorial naming and how it fits into the fundraising process. This is another instance when it is a grave mistake to guess or assume what the donor's desire might be. So, in keeping with our theme, it's time to *Ask about Naming*.

I suggest you first explore the prospect's attitude toward the general practice of naming. We see examples of naming around us every day. But not everyone is a candidate for a naming opportunity. Why is that? The reasons can be very personal, and may be as unique as the person to whom we are speaking. So let's ask.

Begin by asking, "What are your thoughts about naming facilities or programs after benefactors?" Why this question? You'll notice we're not asking "If we agree to name the new school building after you, will you donate lots of money?" *No!* Begin the discussion by exploring the prospect's thoughts in the third person. It's much easier for someone to talk about what others have done, and how they feel about it, than to talk about themselves.

Then, as prospects share their thoughts and observations, we will begin to understand their own preferences.

I can't fully prepare you for the responses you will receive. I know I haven't heard them all...but I have heard a wide variety. For example:

- ◆ "I think it's a great way to recognize people who can do that kind of thing."

- ◆ "Some people like to see their name up in lights."

- ◆ "It can be a good reminder of someone who is generous within the community."

- ◆ Perhaps the most memorable answer I've heard to this question is, "I think the practice is despicable, but it raises money!"

> **From the Donor's Perspective**
>
> "I don't want my name on a building, but I would consider a way to honor my mother (or my wife, my mentor/teacher, etc.)"
>
> **viewpoint**

No matter what the response might be, the question can be the beginning of a very revealing dialogue. You can see—even in the four examples above—that the views can be diverse indeed. And every response calls for a closer look. Your follow-up question may be a simple, brief, "How so?" or a direct, "Why is that?" But if you listen carefully and ask strategically, you will begin to understand the desires, motives, and intent of your donor.

Now is a good time for me to reiterate a foundational principle: Effective fundraising is more about the relationship and less about the transaction. If we are to serve the best and highest interests of our donors, then we must listen to their hearts. And the path doesn't always lead where we want it to go. Because it's about them...not us.

As the conversation continues, you may ask "But what about you? How would you feel about associating your name with this project?"

Here's what I found 'In The Trenches'...

Some people, because of their humility, will initially respond 'no' when asked about a naming opportunity. But they may later take a different position after more in-depth consideration. That's exactly what happened with Randy and Lucille Petrie.

Randy was near retirement after a fruitful career with a global technical enterprise. He made a very generous pledge to the capital campaign for Lucille's alma mater. If he could carefully manage the timing of his gift, his employer's matching grant program would nearly double the impact of his contribution.

I met with Randy for the sole purpose of thanking him and asking "What would be an appropriate way for us to recognize your generosity?" Randy's immediate reply was, "I didn't make the pledge for the purpose of being recognized. I just want you to use the money to build the new building."

After expressing respect for Randy's stance on the issue, we continued our discussion about the progress of the campaign. Soon the topic of naming opportunities came up. I shared a brochure outlining the options for honoring or memorializing a loved one. Before long, Randy's eyes lit up as he began to engage in his own 'possibility thinking.'

The end of the story is that Randy eventually increased his gift and named a conference room in honor of his wife! She was so pleased. Neither of them had anticipated such a tribute. But both thoroughly enjoyed giving back to an institution that had meant so much in their own lives. And they did so in a way that expanded their generosity beyond what they originally intended.

This was all the result of asking, in a very comfortable, conversational way, about naming.

The conversation will be quite different when you're visiting with someone for whom this is a new idea (the majority of the folks you'll talk to) rather than a prospect who has already made several naming gifts. In the latter case, I like to say, "I noticed your name on the public library and the community center conference room. How did you come to those decisions?" And follow up by asking, "Today, do you feel as good about your decisions as you did initially?"

I once asked my friend, Jim Pritchard, why he was so interested in naming opportunities. He named an art studio after his wife. A music library carried the name of a long-time friend who was a church organist. He named the carillon for his deceased first wife. And in each case he allowed his own name to be included on the commemorative plaque.

His response surprised me at first. He said "There are lots of people in this community who retired from the same corporation I did. Scores of them are worth many times more than I am. I want them to see my name and say to themselves, "If Jim Pritchard can do that, so can I!"

Jim helped me see another dimension of the naming consideration. I began to 'get' what Jim had discovered decades earlier. He realized that a naming gift can be inspirational to others. It can motivate people to begin to see themselves doing something they've never done before.

The practice of establishing lasting memorials and tributes isn't something that was 'thought-up' recently. The tradition actually dates back thousands of years. One powerful story from ancient Jewish history provides a pattern for our modern-day practice of naming.

During a time of exile, the nation of Israel crossed the Jordan River to find a place of refuge. During their miraculous passage, God instructed them to take twelve stones from the middle of the riverbed and use them to fashion a memorial. The purpose, He said, was to be significant and permanent.

Joshua, the national leader at that time, went on to explain, "...In the future, when your children ask you, '*What do these stones mean?*' tell them that the flow of the Jordan was cut off before the ark of the covenant of the Lord. When it crossed the Jordan, the waters of the Jordan were cut off. *These stones are to be a memorial to the people of Israel forever.*" (Emphasis added.)

Joshua 4:6-7
New International Version (NIV)

What I especially appreciate about this story is the way it capitalizes on the curiosity of youth to emphasize something of lasting importance.

And when a structure is named commemorating the life and legacy of a giving, caring person, it gives an opportunity to imitate the practice that was established so many years ago. Our children will see the stones (or a bronze sculpture) and ask, "What's that all about?" Then we can explain the person's charitable example and inspire imitation in the heart of an impressionable youngster.

> *Whatever we praise, recognize and reward we will see more of.*
>
> —unknown

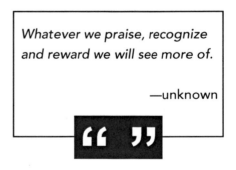

Chapter Ten underscores the danger of *Assuming and Guessing*. Assuming can be problematic, whether we guess in the positive or negative.

Several years ago, an organization I worked with obtained a foundation grant of more than $1 million. I scheduled a meeting to thank the foundation executive, and inquire about a proper way to commemorate the generous gift.

Lots of buildings throughout several states bore the names of the foundation's benefactors. And the magnitude of their gift to our project would easily qualify for a naming opportunity. So I asked, "What would be an appropriate way for us to recognize your donation?"

This seasoned, senior CEO responded with words that I didn't expect—words that I'll never forget. He said, "We like to see our name on buildings, but if you can get more money by using someone else's name... go for the money!"

This funder was truly partnering with the donee to reach the campaign goal and achieve the transformation desired by the organization.

How we say "no" for the donor

He never puts his name on anything.

He won't give the amount necessary to obtain the naming rights.

Sometimes the naming gift is large—sometimes it's small. Consider the brick courtyard. Or a 'seat of honor' in the community concert hall. I once seized the opportunity to honor nine of my own family members by such a gift. Although my gift was modest, it allowed me to perpetuate the legacy of some of the most influential people in my life. In the process I contributed more than what I initially thought I would give. And I was happy to do so. This created a triple win: the donee (the charitable organization), the honorees (my family members), and the donor (me!).

To Recap

Plan of Action

◆ *Who is a prospect* for a naming gift to your organization?

_____

◆ *When* should you call to ask for a meeting?

___/___/___ @ ___:___

◆ *Where* is the most appropriate place to hold this meeting?

_____

◆ *Who* should be part of the discussion?

◆ *What materials* do you need to take along when you meet?

_____

_____

_____

Evaluate your experience:

◆ What was the outcome of the call?

◆ What went well?

◆ What didn't?

◆ How do you feel about the interaction?

◆ What will you repeat in future calls?

◆ What will you avoid in future calls?

◆ What follow-up is required (next step)?

◆ Who will take the next step?

◆ When?

◆ Later, ask the donor for candid feedback/assessment.

Chapter Twenty-Six

Asking about Deciding

IN THIS CHAPTER

···➔ Who is involved in gift decisions?

···➔ How fundraisers assist donors in the decision process

···➔ Cheated out of a wonderful gift opportunity

P erhaps nothing is as frustrating as working through all the aspects of a major gift commitment with prospective donors just to have them 'freeze up' when the time comes to make the final decision. People want to make decisions but some find it very difficult to do so. Mountains of research and countless studies have been conducted, exploring the human decision-making process. Still, it can be very unsettling to act—especially regarding something as important as a major gift decision.

So, how do fundraisers serve donors' best interest in this regard? It helps if we enter into the cultivation process mindful of this potential roadblock. And, before asking for a gift, ask how the decision will be made.

Strategic *listening* follows strategic *asking*.

When we begin working with a new prospect we will be unfamiliar with their decision-making process. Oftentimes the gift they are considering is of a magnitude that they themselves have never experienced.

We can get started by breaking the decision down as follows: "When it's time to make your pledge, who else will be involved in the decision?" In my experience, the responses tend to fall into one of three categories:

1. Nobody

2. Somebody

3. I don't know (or, I haven't thought about it, or, I haven't decided)

From the Donor's Perspective

"I don't make this kind of decision alone. I can't give you an answer today."

Those whose response falls into category one will say something like, "Nobody else is involved...I'll decide this on my own." When you hear this response, it's time to affirm what they're saying before moving on to 'the ask.'

You can proceed by making the following inquiry: "Do I understand that when I present a gift proposal that is just right, you'll make the final decision without further input?"

However, if the response falls into category two, there can be a variety of 'somebodies' who might be involved. Some that I've heard are...

◆ my spouse,

◆ our children,

◆ a business partner,

◆ other family members,

◆ accountant,

◆ pastor/spiritual advisor,

◆ tax attorney,

◆ trust administrator,

◆ foundation board,

◆ investment advisor, and

◆ estate planner.

The possibilities are endless. And, while I've listed the most common 'deciders' I have heard, you'll be astonished at the creativity and variety of responses people will come up with. Keep in mind we're not trying to complicate the process for our prospects, but rather learn how complicated (or simple) their decision process already is.

Upon learning that someone else will be involved in the decision, confirm and probe as follows:

◆ "Once you're comfortable with the proposal, you will present it to your tax attorney for review?" (Affirmation)

◆ "What do you need to feel fully prepared for your meeting?"

◆ "What other materials will you want to have in hand at that time?"

◆ "What else will they need to know to support your decision?"

◆ "Can you foresee any obstacles that might hinder their approval?"

A timely and thoughtful inquiry at this point can illuminate issues early on, giving adequate time to resolve them before they turn into barriers.

Remember, our job is not to make the donors' decisions, but to assist them in arriving at decisions that are exactly right for them. We are there to serve.

Ralph Greer retired from a successful law practice. He and his wife, Amy, were very generous and had supported numerous charities. Ralph was a hard-driving, determined and decisive elderly gentleman. However, he had recently been diagnosed with a serious and advanced form of cancer and was facing his own mortality. Ralph's former business partner, Darrell King—also an attorney, continued to have significant influence in Ralph's major decisions.

The Greers were being cultivated for a leadership gift in a campaign for an organization they had supported generously in the past. Unfortunately, Richard, the executive director, failed to *Ask about Deciding* and, consequently, made what proved to be a grievous error.

With the consent of the Greers, Richard and Darrell were working in tandem, trying to secure a pledge from Ralph and Amy. However, they were so close to the Greers that they couldn't see the calamity that was unfolding in front of them.

Ralph wanted to make a gift of $1.3 million and name a facility in honor of his wife.

Amy wanted to make a gift of $1.3 million and name a facility in honor of her parents.

Darrell wanted the Greers to make a gift of $1.3 million and he didn't care either way about the naming opportunity.

Richard wanted them to make a $1.3 million gift and name a facility that was not of interest to the Greers.

For the most part everyone was in agreement. But there was not a shared understanding of the decision process. Everyone was ready for someone else to make a decision. But no one took the initiative. You could probably guess what happened next...

Time passed.

Everyone waited for someone else to decide.

Ralph's health deteriorated.

Everyone deferred to the others.

More time passed.

Ralph's condition was judged to be 'terminal.'

It became unwise to close the gift agreement because of Ralph's dire condition.

Ralph died.

The gift was never made.

By failing to Ask about Deciding, Ralph and Amy were cheated out of making a magnificent gift during their lifetimes. They missed out on the joy that would have been theirs in paying tribute to their loved ones by naming a facility in their honor. How very sad.

Don't make the same mistakes Darrell and Richard did. If you do, you will come to regret it. Make a firm decision to *Ask about Deciding* before asking for the gift.

To Recap

Plan of Action

◆ *Identify* others who will influence the gift decision.

◆ *Determine* if you should interact with them.

◆ *Outline* the path forward.

◆ *Assign* specific responsibilities for each step.

◆ *Establish* an appropriate timeline.

Evaluate your experience:

◆ What was the outcome of the call?

◆ What went well?

◆ What didn't?

◆ How do you feel about the interaction?

◆ What will you repeat in future calls?

◆ What will you avoid in future calls?

◆ What follow-up is required (next step)?

◆ Who will take the next step?

◆ When?

◆ Later, ask the donor for candid feedback/assessment.

Section F—Asking!

IN THIS SECTION

After getting acquainted with the donor and securing their permission to craft a gift proposal, it's time to ask for the gift. Section F reveals how to enhance donors' enjoyment while they give generously to causes they care deeply about. It also demonstrates how to use a written proposal to make gift requests crystal clear for all who are involved. Readers are equipped to listen actively and respond appropriately, regardless of whether the gift proposal is accepted or not. Guidance is offered on how to prepare for various scenarios by asking several "What if ...?" questions.

There is a huge difference between saying "I'd like you to give $1 million over the next three years" and asking, "Would you consider a gift of $1 million over next three years?"

Our focus throughout this book has been on perfecting the practice of asking for charitable support. We don't want to abandon the main idea at this point in the gift solicitation process, so here's a concise reminder:

Ask. Don't tell.

In Chapters Fifteen and Sixteen we outlined the composition and use of call teams. The value of this arrangement is especially evident at this moment in the solicitation process. Prior to this meeting, each call team member's role was assigned according to the prospect contact plan (see Appendix F). The clarity provided in the plan will provide discipline and unity as we wait for the prospects to respond to the formal gift proposal.

> Successful fundraising is more about the relationship than the transaction.
>
> **principle**

Since we have now climbed up 9 steps on *The 10 Step Staircase*, the hard work is already done. The remaining step, *asking*, should be simple and straightforward. This reinforces one of the principles we have emphasized consistently: Major gifts fundraising is more about the relationship than the transaction.

During previous meetings with the prospective donors, we confirmed the basic elements of the gift proposal and asked for permission to draft a written gift proposal for their review. For a recap, consider the following:

When *Asking about Giving* we learned that Katie observed her parents' practice of regular generosity at church when she was a child. Jason's experience was different. Early in his career he worked for a corporate employer that encouraged volunteerism. This led him to invest his own time in support of the agencies he assisted.

While *Asking about Purpose* the Rutherfords revealed that they are fully supportive of the 'No Boundaries' campaign goals, but would especially like their gift to fund construction of the activity room.

As we *Asked about Form* we discovered that, due to recent gains in the stock market, Katie and Jason are inclined to fund their contribution with appreciated Acme Inc. stock.

Incidentally, our conversation on this topic led to *Asking about Matching*. Katie works for ABC Corporation and her gift of stock will be eligible for their employee matching gift program. With a two-to-one matching rate on gifts of up to $10,000 each year, ABC Corporation will contribute a total of $60,000 over the three-year gift period. And, since Jason serves on the board of Acme Inc. the gift will be eligible for another corporate match of $100,000 annually. These matching programs will extend the impact of the gift by a total of $360,000!

Asking about Amount led to an enlightening discussion of financial priorities. Our generous prospects shared that, although it will be a stretch, if they can have three years to complete their gift they could give at the $1.5 million level.

Later, we *Asked about Timing* and Katie explained that circumstances this year will allow them to contribute the first $400,000 in December. They would then like to split the remainder evenly over the next two calendar years.

As we *Asked about Naming*, the Rutherfords requested that the activity room be named after Betsy Armstrong, Katie's kindergarten teacher, who positively impacted her life by showing selfless kindness, patience and belief in each child's abilities.

While *Asking about Deciding*, Jason and Katie announced that they discuss important philanthropic commitments with each other in order to arrive at a consensus. Afterward, they will seek input from their Certified Financial Planner (CFP) and Certified Public Accountant (CPA) before formalizing their decision.

> *There are no poor givers...only poor askers.*
>
> —Jack Zink
> Industrialist, Philanthropist
> and Racing Enthusiast

When *Asking about Recognition*, the Rutherfords disclosed that, in order to inspire others to "think big" about the No Boundaries campaign, they are open to the idea of their gift amount being shared with others who are also considering a contribution.

DRAFT Gift Proposal

To:	Katie and Jason Rutherford
From:	Healthy Hearts Early Childhood Education Center
Date:	February 11, 20xx
Amount:	$1.5 million (over three years)
Purpose:	No Boundaries campaign
Naming:	Betsy Armstrong Activity Room
Fine Print:	The donation will be fulfilled by stock transfers during each of the next three years. Our facility naming policy requires the board to give final approval to this naming request.
Approvals:	

_____   _____   _____
Katie Rutherford   Date   Jason Rutherford

Katie and Jason readily agreed for us to draw up a proposal. A gift proposal can become infinitely complicated, but it really doesn't need to be. The proposal for the Rutherfords, containing all of the essential requirements, is illustrated above.

At this point we are seeking approval of the basic parameters that were already pre-agreed upon. We can always add complexity to the commitment form if needed. (For a sample of a more formal gift proposal, turn to Appendix E.)

The dialog could go something like this:

Aaron [Jason's 'peer']

Katie...Jason, as you requested during our last meeting, we've put together your proposal based on everything we have discussed so far. Michelle, [the executive director] is going to review the proposal in just a moment, but first I want to say this: Your investment in Healthy Hearts Early Childhood Education Center will forever change the lives of children in our community. On behalf of them, thank you! And I'm confident that your generosity will serve as an example to others...inspiring them to do the same. We are so grateful for your support and excited about how your gift will put hope back into a child's heart. Michelle...

Michelle [the executive director]

As we have visited over the last few weeks you've been very candid in expressing your wishes and priorities regarding this project. We have listened carefully and our proposal includes the specifics and details we heard from you. If we've missed the mark anywhere, please set us straight. Our request is simple: Would you consider a gift of $1.5 million—over the next three years—toward our 'No Boundaries' campaign?

[Hand them each a copy of the one page draft proposal.]

Alternate scripts:

The last time we visited, you indicated how you wanted to be involved in our soon-to-be-announced 'No Boundaries' campaign. We have drafted a proposal based on the things we heard and would like to review it with you.

I would really appreciate the opportunity to go through this with you to see if there is anything I may have missed. Let's look at this together.

Discipline

Refine the skill of knowing when to simply be quiet and listen.

Now is the time to be quiet and listen. Be mindful that the proposal consists entirely of elements that have already been discussed and agreed to (informally). There is nothing new here. It is essential for the call team to wait patiently for the donors to scan the proposal. Then, when they raise questions or issues, respond appropriately.

Here are some of the mistakes that are commonly made at this time:

◆ Keep talking. (You asked a question. Let them answer. But give them all the time they need to process your request and come to a full understanding of the proposal.)

◆ Talk them out of their good decision. (Yes, this really happens! The solicitor will say, "You don't have to do this if you don't want to." They already know that, and we've provided ample opportunities for them to decline previously. Just listen.)

◆ Become negative. (Strangely enough, a member of the call team may blurt out, "Some people aren't as enthusiastic in their support as you." This causes the donor to wonder, "Should I really be doing this? What do they know that I don't?")

◆ Rehash old issues that have already been resolved. (Someone asks, "Are you still upset—or concerned, or curious, or confused, or unhappy, or unsure—about _____?" Rest assured that if this is the case they can raise the issue themselves.)

◆ Introduce new issues that this donor has no (previous) stake in. ("Do you know why U.S. Manufacturing has stopped sponsoring our annual golf tournament?" Our place is to respond to the Rutherfords' reservations, not create them.)

If the donors are ready to approve the proposal, ask them to sign it and let the celebration begin! They have taken a step that they have been moving toward from the time the project was first introduced to them. Rejoice! Thank them. Now is the time to 'lock arms' and move forward together.

> **From the Donor's Perspective**
>
> "Wow – these people have really been listening to us! Their proposal is exactly in line with everything we had in mind. This will be easy for us to say 'yes' to."
>
> **viewpoint**

The next section provides guidance on how to say 'thank you.' After expressing your gratitude, you will want to ask this important question: "Who else should we be talking to about this project?" (See Chapter Thirty, *Asking "Who Else?"*)

To Recap

Plan of Action

◆ *Who is ready* to be asked for a major gift?

_____

◆ Decide *when* you should call to ask for a meeting.
___/___/___ @ ___:___

◆ *Where* is the most appropriate place to hold this meeting?

_____

◆ *Who* will join you when you meet with the prospect?

_____

◆ *What materials* do you need to take along when you meet?

_____

_____

_____

◆ Not ready yet? What needs to happen before making a formal gift proposal? Create a specific list:

What is to be done? _____

Who will do it? _____

When? _____

Evaluate your experience:

◆ What was the outcome of the call?

◆ What went well?

◆ What didn't?

◆ How do you feel about the interaction?

◆ What will you repeat in future calls?

◆ What will you avoid in future calls?

◆ What follow-up is required (next step)?

◆ Who will take the next step?

◆ When?

◆ Later, ask the donor for candid feedback/assessment.

Chapter Twenty-Seven

Listening and Responding

IN THIS CHAPTER

···→ How to listen actively after submitting a gift proposal

···→ Responding in a constructive manner regardless of the donor's decision

···→ What it means to 'throw a brick through the window'

A s you master the principles, practices and disciplines described within this book you will be hearing "Yes!" more frequently. Be prepared to accept the generous gifts that are offered and celebrate with your new donors.

At times, however, you will encounter other replies. You should be equally prepared and appropriately responsive if the answer is not an immediate "Yes." No matter how careful we have been in our cultivation and preparation, there are times when this happens. But regardless of the disappointment you may feel, be reminded that it is OK. After all...we're asking, not telling.

Managing your own expectations

The three most common responses to a skillfully delivered request for a charitable contribution are:

1. Yes
2. No
3. Not now

Be prepared to extend the conversation long enough to discover the basis for any hesitation.

Once 'the ask' has been made, it's important to listen carefully to the prospect's response. And the only way that can occur is for everyone on the call team to stop talking.

What if it is quiet? That's OK. For a long time? Just wait. Remember—you asked. And it's impolite to ask a question and not wait for a reply. Discipline yourself to be patient... especially at this moment.

The words that are spoken next will be full of meaning. Listen strategically.

Since there may be as many different replies as there are people, I'm not going to give you a menu of responses. This is a very personal dialogue so I want to prepare you to focus intently on what your prospect has to say.

The face and hands and eyes of your prospect will tell you as much as the words you hear. And as you observe...and listen...be prepared to actively confirm what you hear.

If a smile appears and the donor picks up a pen and signs the gift proposal—celebrate! Thank the donor for their generous support. (See Chapter Twenty-Nine, *Thanking*, for more specifics.)

Perhaps something has changed in the prospects' situation and now just isn't the time for them to make a major gift decision. If that's the case, find out what would need to change in order for them to be ready to make a decision.

If the response is reluctant or unenthusiastic, inquire further to discover what it means. For more in-depth treatment, be sure to check out Chapter Twenty-Eight, *What if the Answer is 'No'?*

Early in my fundraising career, I received some sage advice from a seasoned senior consultant who had become a mentor to me. It had to do with how we react to a donor whose response to our request for support is less than what we had hoped for. His advice: "Never throw a brick through their window."

Now, I can't say I have ever been inclined to respond to a gift prospect in this fashion. It seems a bit extreme to me. But the sentiment is right on target. This is no time to abandon your poise and professionalism. Remember our 'Big 3'? We specialize in relationships, not just transactions. It's about the mission, not about me. I'm in it for the long-term, not just today.

While a decision to not fund a request for philanthropic support may be the first response of your prospect...it need not be the last. My experience is that, if we handle the situation graciously, a decline may be the first step toward a positive response to our next request.

Resist any impulse you may have to 'throw a brick through the window' of prospects who choose not to fund your request.

practical tip

A grant maker told me about a particularly unpleasant conversation she once had with someone representing an organization her foundation had once funded. This dialogue took place via telephone. It had been about one year since the previous grant was made. No additional request had been submitted. The exchange went something like this:

Foundation Executive: "Hello."

Development Director: "I was calling to find out when we would receive our grant this year."

Foundation Executive: "I'm sorry; I don't recall seeing a request from you."

Development Director: "We did that last year. You approved the grant and we need money again this year. When can I pick up my check?"

Foundation Executive: "No need to come by. We won't be making another grant anytime soon. Good bye."

This story was relayed to me months after it happened. It was so clear in my friend's memory that I could see her pulse quicken as she retold the experience. "I couldn't believe the audacity!" she exclaimed. Fortunately, this scenario is the exception—not the rule. But, I think this must have been what my mentor had in mind with the term "throwing a brick through their window." I'm not sure this relationship would have been damaged more if a window had literally been shattered!

The story reveals a mindset that is too commonplace in the nonprofit sector. It's an entitlement mentality that somehow views charitable support as a right to be asserted, rather than a privilege to be earned. Always keep in mind that we're talking about gifts. A gift is freely given at the sole discretion of the giver.

The words we use sometimes betray a wrong view of giving. I hear development directors talk about waiting for a donor to 'pay their pledge' or ask when the contributor is going to 'give us what they owe us.' Or, similar to the exchange above, inquire 'When can I pick up my check?' 'When will you pay our invoice?' Ad infinitum...ad nauseum.

This exact terminology is common and appropriate in business practice. But it vividly illustrates the contrast between a transaction (*Pay what you owe*) and a relationship (*We appreciate your generous pledge*).

So how should a fundraising professional graciously respond to a decision that falls short of the request? Let me offer four steps.

First, *clarify* your understanding. You can ask, "You're saying you cannot approve the proposal at this time?" Or "Does the decision timetable make you feel uncomfortable?" Perhaps the question is, "Is there a problem with the amount?" Or, "Have I missed something?"

Next, *affirm* the prospect's decision. Be sure they know you realize this to be their choice, not yours. And underscore your commitment to the relationship.

Third, *inquire* far enough to assure that you understand which parts of your proposal were on target (acceptable) and which were not (unacceptable).

Finally, come to agreement with the prospect regarding the future steps you will take together and a suitable timetable.

In closing, for more in-depth treatment of the subject, you may wish to refer back to Chapter Thirteen, *The Essential Practice of Listening* and, Chapter Fourteen, *Responding in a Manner that Engages.*

What to say:

If your prospect is unsure about when would be a good time to make a gift decision, announce something along these lines:

"As soon as the condition changes please give me a call so we can visit further on this topic."

Or ask, "If I don't hear from you in the next six weeks would you mind if I touch base with you?"

 practical tip

To Recap

Plan of Action

◆ *To whom* will you submit your next gift proposal?

_____

◆ How will you *react* if they approve your request?

_____

◆ How will you *respond* if they deny your request?

_____

◆ Choose a friend or colleague with whom you can role play and *practice* your replies.

_____

◆ Decide *when* you should call to ask for a meeting.
   ___/___/___ @ ___:___

◆ *Where* is the most appropriate place to hold this meeting?

_____

◆ *Who* will join you when you meet with the prospect?

_____

◆ *What materials* do you need to take along when you meet?

_____

_____

_____

Evaluate your experience:

◆ What was the outcome of the call?

◆ What went well?

◆ What didn't?

◆ How do you feel about the interaction?

◆ What will you repeat in future calls?

◆ What will you avoid in future calls?

◆ What follow-up is required (next step)?

◆ Who will take the next step?

◆ When?

◆ Later, ask the donor for candid feedback/assessment.

Chapter Twenty-Eight

What if the Answer is 'No'?

IN THIS CHAPTER

···→ Getting over 'No'

···→ Is it 'No' or 'Not now'?

···→ What happens next?

···→ When?

N

o matter how thoughtful, skillful, patient and deliberate the fundraiser has been, there is a possibility that a gift proposal may not be accepted by the prospect. To become well-rounded in your skills, anticipate the possibility that your request may be 'declined' and be ready to respond appropriately.

Fundraisers pour themselves into their work and can easily take it very personally when the gift proposal is not accepted. There can be any number of reasons for non-acceptance, and it is human nature to interpret the response in the most negative light. This will inevitably leave one feeling discouraged or defeated. You may even be tempted to respond in an unprofessional manner.

One contributing factor is the terminology we use. For example, the use of the term 'rejection,' as in, "Katie and Jason rejected our gift proposal!" would cause anyone to feel badly.

Let's take a closer look at the word 'reject.' The dictionary includes some very negative and emotionally charged terms:

  1. to refuse to have;

  2. to refuse to accept;

  3. to discard as useless or unsatisfactory; or

  4. to cast out or off.

Ouch! It hurts just to read those words.

Instead, let me suggest a different term, 'decline.' The same dictionary describes a negative response, but without the hurtful connotation:

  1. to withhold or deny consent to do;

  2. to express inability or reluctance to accept; or

  3. to refuse with courtesy.

The word 'decline' still communicates non-acceptance, but it's not as hurtful as 'rejection.'

My first recommendation is that you view a negative response to your gift proposal as 'declined' rather than 'rejected.'

Earlier we stated that the process of gift solicitation is all about the donor and not about the fundraiser. That same reality exists at this point. The donor's response to a gift proposal is about the donor. It's not about the fundraiser.

It's inevitable to be disappointed, especially when you have carefully climbed all 10 Steps on the Staircase, and now discover that the door is marked 'No' instead of 'Yes.' To stay true to form, we must continue even now to build the relationship by *asking*.

As soon as the prospect communicates a decline of the proposal, acknowledge their response and then find out what is behind the 'No.' For instance, respond by saying, "I hear you saying you are not inclined to make a pledge at this time. Thank you for your thoughtful consideration and your candor. May I ask what part of the proposal is unsatisfactory?" You are sincerely requesting feedback, just as you did in your earlier cultivation calls.

This is an important time to listen actively. You want to learn if the response is 'No,' 'Not now,' 'Not ever,' or something else.

Listen to find out if 'No' means...

1. No today. No tomorrow. No always. The prospect's philanthropic priorities are elsewhere. Period.

2. No—to the amount. We asked about the idea of a 'major' gift. The prospect might consider a gift but it doesn't rise to the level of 'major' in her mind. This may be the time to delve into the donor's concept of a major gift.

3. No—to the gift. "I would consider volunteering but I'm not ready to write a check." Conventional wisdom tells us that 'investment follows involvement.' (See the The Donor Development Cycle on the next page.) People are more likely to make a monetary gift to a charitable cause after being personally involved in some aspect of the mission. In my case, I'm more open to a request for a contribution to the regional food bank after I have spent three hours serving hot meals to hungry homeless people, than if I simply receive a letter in the mail while watching Monday Night Football at home.

4. No—to the project. Each donor has a unique set of priorities and preferences. I have known people who would give sacrificially to fund a scholarship, but would not contribute ten dollars toward a new athletic field. Remember, we're asking people to contribute from their 'heart.' If their heart is shaped differently than this particular project, let's willingly honor their preference.

After learning all you can about why the request was 'declined,' be deliberate in keeping the door open to future interaction by a gracious

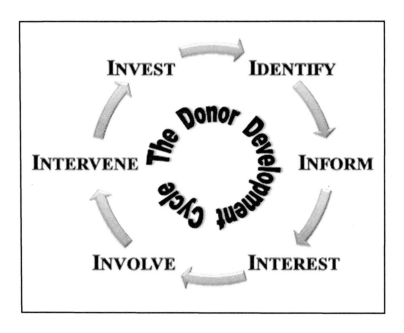

response such as, "I would love to stay in contact with you and keep you informed as other developments emerge at Healthy Hearts. Would that be OK?"

Be respectful of the prospect's decision. Realize that today's negative response may be the first step toward acceptance of a future request.

Also remember; this prospect will be talking to other prospects, funders, volunteers and constituents of your organization. The way you respond will make an indelible impression on the prospect. That image will be conveyed to others in numerous ways. Your grace and professionalism will be portrayed to countless other individuals. Likewise, your response will be relayed to others if you are tactless or unprofessional. Your choice will determine what your legacy will be.

After you leave the donor meeting, give yourself permission to grieve the loss. You worked long and hard with the anticipation of a different outcome. Don't wallow in self-pity, but give yourself time to get over the disappointment.

The true measure of success in fundraising is bringing about an informed decision that is appropriate for the donor's circumstances. From page one on, we have acknowledged that *ultimately the donor decides* whether to make a gift...or not. And since the decision really does belong to the donor, our place is to accept and respect it.

Then, I say, "Celebrate!" You assisted your prospect in making an appropriate informed decision. The decision is different than hoped for, but you did your part. Now it's time to work with other prospective donors.

> *Adversity causes some men to break; others to break records.*
>
> —William Arthur Ward

Learn what you can from this experience and become a better person for it. It has been said that there is an island of opportunity in the middle of every ocean of difficulty. Seize this opportunity as you continue your quest to Master the Art of Conversational Fundraising!

To Recap

Plan of Action

♦ *Identify the donor* whose answer to your gift proposal is 'No'.

♦ Grieve the loss.

♦ What lesson can you learn from this particular decline?

♦ Decide how you should celebrate the conclusion of this prospect solicitation.

♦ *Determine* which prospect you should begin to focus on now.

Evaluate your experience:

♦ How do you feel about your interaction with this prospect?

♦ What will you repeat in future calls?

♦ What will you avoid in future calls?

♦ What follow-up is required (next step)?

♦ Who will take the next step?

♦ When?

♦ Later, ask the donor for candid feedback/assessment.

Section G—After the Ask

IN THIS SECTION

Section G offers advice on the four topics that must be covered after the donor has decided upon a specific gift. Fundraising personnel will learn how to interact with donors in ways that will enhance future gift solicitations.

The 'ask' has been made and the proposal was accepted. You listened carefully and responded graciously. But the job is not done. There are four more subjects to address after asking for the pledge. The topics are:

◆ Thanking,

◆ Referrals,

◆ Recognition, and

◆ Repetition.

The first two items are time sensitive. The time to say "Thank you," and ask "Who else?" is now.

Chapter Twenty-Nine

Thanking

IN THIS CHAPTER

- ⋯➔ Not the time to hold back
- ⋯➔ Saying it and meaning it
- ⋯➔ Employing the Inclusion Principle

In Chapter Twenty-Eight we outlined the conversation that might occur if the response to our 'ask' is "No" or "Not now." If you fully implement the Art of Conversational Fundraising as outlined on these pages you're going to hear negative responses much less often.

Instead you'll be hearing an enthusiastic "Yes!" more frequently. Immediately it will be natural and appropriate to say, "Thank you."

This is not the time to be shy or evasive. If ever you have been tempted to blurt out a response, this is the time to give in!

The donors' commitment is so intense at this time, and their enthusiasm so strong, that they and solicitors alike are often moved with deep emotion.

Whatever your personal expression of gratitude may be: Enjoy the moment.

If you are inclined to 'do the happy dance,' then dance!

If you're the 'strong silent type,' indulge in a moment of quiet satisfaction!

If you are a 'crier,' feel free to weep with joy!

But please observe this one admonition. Don't let the moment pass without looking each of the donors straight in the eyes and saying a clear, sincere, heartfelt "Thank you."

Personally, I like to express gratitude on behalf of those who will ultimately benefit from the gift by saying, "On behalf of the hundreds of children who will learn and play in the 'Betsy Armstrong Activity Room' please accept my deepest gratitude. Your legacy of generosity will make a positive impact on generation after generation. Thank you."

There will be times when you will not be present when the gift or pledge is made. Don't let that deter you from an appropriate expression of thanks. These situations actually open up avenues for even more intentional and creative ways of thanking.

During my time in higher education I worked with an elegant, retired corporate executive whose health was failing, keeping her homebound. Linda Tipton had a real passion for healthcare education. She generously funded the start-up of a nursing program and subsequently made annual gifts to the scholarship fund.

Since Linda was unable to come to campus, I conspired to take the appreciation to her. With the assistance of the Nursing Department chair and one of the graduates, I obtained a framed, signed photograph of the entire class of nurses.

I made an appointment to visit Linda in her home at a time that was convenient to her. Without divulging the full purpose of my visit, I playfully told Linda, "I want to introduce you to someone special."

When the appointed day arrived, Jennifer (one of the graduates) and I knocked at the front door of Linda' home. With a broad smile on my face, I introduced Jennifer to Linda as, "One of the students who has benefited directly from your generosity." The two made an immediate bond and chatted at length about how the nursing scholarship had enabled a deserving young lady to prepare for a career in health care. Linda exhibited a liveliness that afternoon that I had never witnessed before.

But the highlight of the afternoon came when I told Linda, "Jennifer and I have a special presentation for you." On that cue, Jennifer reached into a colorful gift bag, removed the framed, signed photograph of her classmates, and gently placed it in Linda's feeble hands. The pride and satisfaction on Linda's face brought tears to my eyes.

From the words and reactions I observed that day, you would think Jennifer and I were the donors, and Linda was the recipient. And, in a sense, the roles were reversed. Everyone in the room that day was deeply moved by the celebration of philanthropy.

There will be other ways to recognize and thank the donor, but the first spontaneous acknowledgement may be the most important.

In addition, be sure to take the following steps:

> ### The Inclusion Principle
>
> When sincere, purposeful 'thanking' takes place, *everyone* participates in the philanthropic experience!

practical tip

1. The agency CEO should write or call that same day, or the next, with a personal expression of gratitude.

2. The 'peer' member of the call team should do the same.

3. In the case of an outright gift, a formal donation receipt should be sent within twenty-four hours.

4. If the commitment is a pledge, send a pledge confirmation letter within twenty-four hours.

As all of this thanking is taking place, don't overlook considerations of confidentiality. There are times when a donor wishes to keep the peer solicitor from knowing how much their gift is. This may be due to any number of personal considerations. In this case, the volunteer (peer) will be saying 'thank you' for a gift or pledge without being aware of the exact amount of the commitment. That's okay. Always exercise discretion. And if you're unsure about the donor's wishes, ask. (You knew I was going suggest that, didn't you?)

To Recap

Plan of Action

♦ *Identify the donor* you need to thank.

_____

♦ *Who* should thank the donor?

_____

♦ *How?*

_____

♦ Decide when you should call to ask for a meeting.

___/___/___ @ ___:___

♦ *Where* is the most appropriate place to hold this meeting?

_____

◆ *What materials* do you need to take?

_____

_____

_____

Evaluate your experience:

◆ What was the outcome of the call?

◆ What went well?

◆ What didn't?

◆ How do you feel about the interaction?

◆ What will you repeat in future calls?

◆ What will you avoid in future calls?

◆ What follow-up is required (next step)?

◆ Who will take the next step?

◆ When?

◆ Later, ask the donor for candid feedback/assessment.

Chapter Thirty

Asking "Who Else?"

IN THIS CHAPTER

···→ Learn when to ask for referrals

···→ Understand why the timing matters so much

···→ Discover how to ask respectfully and delicately

···→ Prepare to follow through on names that are offered

I mmediately when a major gift decision is made, something amazing happens. The donor's mind automatically begins to think of ways to assure that the investment proves to be a wise one. The donor is excited about solving an important issue and wants to see the promised results without delay.

At this precise moment, fundraisers should make a sincere observation followed by a strategic question such as, "Katie and Jason, I can see you are thrilled about the commitment you just made. *Who else should we be talking to about a gift for this project?*" Or, stated differently, "You just made a generous commitment to the mission of Healthy Hearts Early Childhood Education Center. How do you feel about your decision?"

followed by asking, "Who do you know that might enjoy the same sense of fulfillment you are experiencing right now?"

Don't rush the conversation at this point. It's a new topic for the donor, whose mind has been intently focused elsewhere. It can take a moment for them to 'shift gears,' but be patient.

When they do respond, here's what you can expect. Approximately 80 percent of the names offered will already be on your 'radar screen.' The remaining 20 percent will be new prospects.

Express sincere appreciation for the mention of names that are already on your prospect list. Inquire about linkage by asking, "What is your connection with her?" or "Who would be the best person to approach him with a gift request?"

When a new name is mentioned be ready to take the next step immediately with a reply along these lines, "I don't know her. Would you be willing to introduce us?"

This is a priceless 'stewardship moment.'

After asking this question, wait quietly and attentively and allow the new donor to roll up his sleeves and go to work. I am always amazed at how quickly people will accept the challenge

---

From the Donor's Perspective

"I feel so good about contributing! I want my friends, family members, business associates, etc. to have an opportunity to do the same."

Don't overlook 'Stewardship Moments'

One way to show appreciation is to allow the donor to be personally involved in the success of your organization. Your request for a donor to introduce you to another prospect will draw the donor closer to the charity, while bringing a new individual into the mix at the same time.

when we simply ask and then sit back and allow them to use their own creativity and resourcefulness.

Once I asked Jeff Sager, a retired corporate executive, "Who else should we be talking to?" He began to work as diligently on the fundraising project as the paid staff. Jeff had a wealth of relationships from his thirty-five year career in the business world. He had almost unlimited time to dedicate to the task. And his unrestrained enthusiasm for the project was powerful and convincing.

In a few days' time Jeff had arranged meetings with corporate and philanthropic leaders who had been unreachable previously. He arranged an after-hours reception at his country club, invited scores of his former clients, and picked up the tab for the entire event. As a result of Jeff's efforts, tens of thousands of dollars were contributed—in a very short time—by people who simply would not have been reached otherwise. They, in turn, began to follow Jeff's example with their own respective networks and resources.

It was as if an entire army of fundraisers had been commissioned for the project—and they were all working gratis! It began with a simple question.

Not everyone responds like Jeff Sager and takes such a personal interest in the success of a new project. But some do. Conversely, when we don't ask "Who else?" we can expect to get no referrals.

What can you do if the new donor doesn't think of any names to suggest? I like to keep a list of my 'Ten Most Wanted' prospects and make a specific ask in this situation. For example, ask "Do you know Ray White? Do you know someone who does? We've been trying to make a connection with him and haven't come up with a go-between yet."

Inquiring about a specific person helps bring focus to the conversation. It provides an example of the kind of information you are seeking and often spurs a flood of names that seemed non-existent just moments earlier.

How we say "No" for Donors

Thinking that their generosity ends when they make a gift or pledge. If we don't ask for referrals we cannot reach out to donors' friends, associates and family members.

warning!

Marlin Hays was a passionate supporter, dedicated board member and generous donor to his alma mater. The gift he made to the university's capital campaign was sacrificial and inspiring. When I asked him, "Who else should we be talking to," he didn't have an immediate answer. The true measure of his enthusiasm for the project was revealed, however, when he called me several days later.

Marlin was almost breathless with excitement when he exclaimed, "I've found another donor for our campaign!" He went on to explain, "Before my retirement, I worked forty-two years for a public utility that didn't have an employee matching gift program. Several years ago another corporation bought the company. Likewise, they had no policy of matching gifts. But today I learned that the second company was just acquired by a huge conglomerate that does have a matching gift plan!"

What not to say:

"We'd like to hit up your friends for money also. Can I have your contact list?" This presumptuous request can cause a donor to second guess the wisdom of their own gift. Savvy fundraisers will remain focused, discreet and considerate when asking for referrals.

 **practical tip**

"But that's not the best part," Marlin continued. "The new owner will match gifts made by retirees from all previous companies!" I couldn't help getting caught up in his enthusiasm. "That's terrific," I replied. "This will double the impact of your contribution. How wonderful!"

Before I could say more, Marlin interrupted with, "No – it gets even better! The matching gift rate is three to one!" I could hardly believe what I was hearing, so I quizzed Marlin to be sure I had all the facts straight. Later he obtained the contact information for the corporate gifts office and they confirmed every detail of Marlin's claim about the new employee/retiree matching contribution policy.

As a result, Marlin worked all the harder to contribute as many of his resources as possible to leverage more and more dollars toward the university he loved so much.

Someone might say the triple gift match would have happened anyway. Perhaps that is true. But it didn't. And I wouldn't gamble on the possibility. Make a regular discipline of asking donors for referrals as soon as they make their own gift.

You'll be amazed at the results.

To Recap

Plan of Action

- ◆ Which donors should you approach to ask the 'Who else?' question?
  _____

- ◆ Should your contact be made in person or by phone? (It's best not to make this request in a letter or email.)
  _____

- ◆ *When* should you get in touch with the donor(s)?
  ___/___/___ @ ___:___

- ◆ What do you need to do to prepare?

  _____

  _____

  _____

Evaluate your experience:

◆ What was the outcome of the call?

◆ What went well?

◆ What didn't?

◆ How do you feel about the interaction?

◆ What will you repeat in future calls?

◆ What will you avoid in future calls?

◆ What follow-up is required (next step)?

◆ Who will take the next step?

◆ When?

◆ Later, ask the donor for candid feedback/assessment.

Chapter Thirty-One

Asking about Recognition

IN THIS CHAPTER

···→ Reasons to recognize donors

···→ Examples of intentional and spontaneous gift recognition

···→ How and why to *Ask about Recognition*

G ift recognition is a delicate topic. Some donors want it. Some don't. It's a very personal matter.

When donors make gifts at a level that is significant for them, and perhaps transformational for the organization, it provides an opportunity to cultivate the relationship by giving special recognition. Rather than guess what would be fitting—*ask*. One of the ways I like to ask is, "What would be an appropriate way for us to acknowledge your gift?" or, "How could we thank you for your generosity?"

Never guess. Always ask.

practical tip

Early in my fundraising career I attended a funders' forum that consisted of corporate and foundation decision makers who described their respective granting policies, practices and preferences. At the end of the program the floor was opened for questions. One attendee asked the panel "What do you like and dislike when it comes to thanking you for your support?" I'll never forget the response given by a foundation trustee: "The answer will vary greatly from one organization to the next," he said. "Since you don't know, but we do—*ask us.*"

When he said these words, it inspired me beyond what I could have imagined at the time. Anything short of following his advice puts you right back at a place you are working hard to avoid—guessing. I am so thankful for such sage advice!

How we *guess* for the donor

Whenever major gift recognition decisions are made without consulting the donor, we are *guessing* on their behalf. We make well-intentioned but arbitrary comments like, "Plaques are a great way to say 'thanks' let's give everybody a nice one." Or, "He never wants his name mentioned. Let's just list him as 'anonymous.'" Or, "She already put her parents' name on another building. She would have no interest in doing that again."

warning!

There are many reasons for prominently recognizing charitable gifts. Sometimes recognition is for the purpose of giving personal gratification to the donor. Other times its purpose is to capture the attention of new potential donors and inspire them to give also. Frequently donors wish to pay tribute to loved ones, teachers, mentors or business associates.

Lynal Root entered college in the late 1940s, intending to earn a degree in theology and become a pastor. His younger brother wanted to do the same. Unfortunately, hard times overcame the family and it was impossible for both boys to continue their education. In an act of true selflessness, Lynal decided to suspend his studies and enter the work force, allowing his brother to remain in school. Perhaps Lynal could reenroll later and finish his degree at another time.

As you might imagine, 'another time' never came. Lynal married, began a family of his own and pursued a career in the corporate world.

As it turned out, Lynal reengineered the supply chain management system for McDonald's worldwide. His methodology was adopted by entrepreneurs all across the globe—earning literal fortunes for scores of men and women. Lynal left a legacy that inspired people all around the world. He didn't do it from a pulpit; his 'sermons' were preached from a corporate platform.

I became aware of Lynal's legacy only after he died. One of his business colleagues contacted me and asked if he could start a scholarship endowment in Lynal's name to help others achieve what Lynal had been unable to do for himself.

When it came time to honor Lynal's legacy, it was natural that grateful beneficiaries of his business acumen would do so in a conspicuous way. Lynal would be so gratified to realize that his business partners were opening doors of opportunity for successive generations of underprivileged youth. Sometimes, as in Lynal's legacy, donor recognition is spontaneous. But, spontaneous or deliberate, gift recognition—tastefully done—serves as a catalyst for even more generosity.

> **Don't Ignore the Donor's Wishes**
>
> The desires of the donor must not be ignored. If someone sincerely does not wish to be recognized for their gift, respect their preference. Conversely, if they have some openness to the idea, don't misinterpret an initial decline as the final answer. This is an important dimension of the relational aspect of fundraising.
>
> **warning!**

Over many years of *Asking about Recognition,* I have noticed that donors' first response is most often, "We didn't make our gift to be recognized. We gave to achieve the objectives of the campaign." It requires a delicate balance to be respectful of donors' wishes and still explore ways to appropriately recognize their generosity.

They may wish to leave a testament about their own lives or pay tribute to someone else.

Back to Royce and Helen McCormick. You will recall their story from Chapter Twenty-Two, *Asking about Form.* They funded a charitable gift annuity by donating a rental house.

Responding to objections

When donors say, "We don't want to be thanked..." or "My husband and I want 100 percent of our gift to go to..." it might, or might not, be a genuine objection. Donors are emphatic about not having the impact of their gift eroded by spending it to acknowledge their generosity. But most contributors are open to appropriate, tasteful expressions of gratitude. Engage them directly in the discussion of how, when and where they will be thanked, and who will be in the audience.

 practical tip

---

After their gift had been formalized and all the papers had been signed, they savored the joy of "making a larger gift than we ever imagined." So I asked, "What would be an appropriate way for us to say 'thank you' for your gift?"

I think you'll catch a glimpse of their true character with Helen's first reply, "I think we should be saying 'Thank you' to the university for all they have done for us!"

But Royce picked up the conversation and asked, "Would it be possible to name one of the seats in the new chapel for Helen?" To put Royce's request in context, you need to know that at that very time the university was concluding a major capital campaign. One of the wrap-up strategies was a 'seat of honor' promotion allowing people to name a seat in the new auditorium in memory or honor of a loved one. The gift portion of the McCormick's annuity would have covered the cost of dozens of 'seats of honor.' Royce's unpretentious request was an accurate reflection of his humble character and gentle spirit. This was a great opportunity to express heartfelt appreciation for a generous gift that had been so willingly made.

Since I was personally acquainted with each member of Royce and Helen's family, I suggested an alternative: "Would it be OK if we named a 'seat of honor' for each of your children, their spouses and both of you?"

My offer extended well beyond what Royce and Helen would have ever proposed. Eventually, after gently helping them overcome their initial reluctance, I arranged to do just that.

> **From the Donor's Perspective**
>
> "Please don't spend a lot of money just to thank me for something I really want to do."
>
> **viewpoint**

Our dialog about recognition that day was not 'textbook' by any means. It was conversational at every level. The result was that everyone involved can point back to that moment and recall a mutually rewarding, sincere celebration of pure philanthropy.

It is important for every organization to develop its own gift recognition policies, framework, and structure. Be careful, however, that the policies are not too rigid. Assure that there is enough room to make the recognition personal. And be sure to have fun in the process!

Gift recognition can become intricate when it involves a group rather than an individual. Consider the following scenario. While some charitable foundations have specific policies dictating how their donations are to be recognized, this was not the case with the Griffin Foundation. They made the first seven-figure pledge toward a campaign to build a music performance hall. At a later time, an in-depth conversation began like this: "Your gift has been transformational for our organization. How can we

> **Stewardship Principle**
>
> Acknowledgment is primarily about the giver not the receiver.
>
>  **practical tip**

help others remember your generosity?" After discussing a handful of possibilities, it was agreed that the auditorium would be named for the family who had established the foundation, but were long since deceased.

As fitting as this designation was, it did not directly affirm the pivotal role played by the foundation trustees. Rather than risk offending them by ignoring their role, arrangements were made to give the trustees recognition at the time the facility was dedicated. At the appropriate time in the program the trustees were invited to stand before the assembled crowd. They were thanked for their inspirational role, and given symbolic 'front door keys' attached to commemorative medallions as an expression of gratitude for their influential action. Each of the trustees expressed personal appreciation for the tribute, as well as indicating approval that the funds were not 'squandered' on thanking them.

> **Dual recognition**
>
> Recognize generosity collectively at the charitable organization's site, and individually in a form that is personally suitable to the donor. Remember: One size doesn't fit all.
>
>  practical tip

To Recap

Plan of Action

◆ *Identify the donor* with whom you need to meet to ask about recognition.

_____

◆ Decide when you should call to ask for a meeting.
___/___/___ @ ___:___

◆ *Where* is the most appropriate place to hold this meeting?

_____

◆ *Who* will join you when you meet with the prospect?

_____

◆ *What materials* do you need to take along when you meet?

_____

_____

_____

Evaluate your experience:

◆ What was the outcome of the call?

◆ What went well?

◆ What didn't?

◆ How do you feel about the interaction?

◆ What will you repeat in future calls?

◆ What will you avoid in future calls?

◆ What follow-up is required (next step)?

◆ Who will take the next step?

◆ When?

◆ Later, ask the donor for candid feedback/assessment.

Chapter Thirty-Two

Asking about Asking *Again*

IN THIS CHAPTER

···➤ Choosing your assumptions and managing expectations

···➤ Donor contributions: A onetime occurrence or a continuing cycle?

···➤ Revisiting *The 10 Step Staircase*

W hen do we begin to think and talk in terms of the next contribution? I would suggest that it be a *constant* practice. Asked differently, is there anyone you would want to approach with the idea that they contribute to a worthy cause *only once*? If the cause for which you are raising money is worth perpetuating, always keep the door open for ongoing support.

As we have stated from the beginning, we want to be conversational rather than confrontational. This applies equally to the idea of giving again. If it is introduced early on, donors will have an opportunity to warm up to the topic long before it is time to ask for their renewed support.

Myth versus Reality

It's a *mistake* to believe that donors will not contribute again after already giving to our charity. The reality is this, 'The best source for a gift is someone who has already given.'

practical tip

Eventually, when their pledge is paid in full, we want to encourage donors to begin thinking in serious terms about their next contribution. This is what we mean by *Asking about Asking Again.*

People in the fundraising field use the term, 'gift renewal' to describe the process of seeking contributions from those who have donated in the past. Research indicates that the best source for a contribution is someone who has already given. Yet this runs counter to our 'common sense' that suggests, "We can't ask Max and Dorothy for a donation. They have already given."

Expectations are most effective when communicated in advance of performance. Don't surprise donors by suddenly approaching them with a request for renewed support. Introduce the concept early on. For

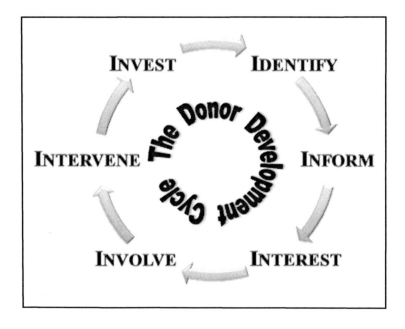

example, soon after a pledge is made toward a building campaign announce: "After the new community center is completed we will be seeking operational support. I hope you'll consider helping out at that time."

> **How we say "no" for the donor**
>
> "We can't ask someone who already donated to give again."
>
> **warning!**

This is what we refer to as 'stewardship' or 'donor relations.' The example we are using is a three-year pledge for a major capital fund raising

> *Expect* donors to continue their support.
>
> **recommendation**

campaign. We certainly don't want to turn around the next day and make a request for another contribution. Rather, I like to view a three year pledge as an invitation from the donor to spend those three years cultivating their next gift.

Sometime after the gift proposal has been approved and we have thanked the donor, asked "Who else?" and asked about recognition, we should introduce the idea of *Asking about Asking Again*.

At some point each person must choose the assumptions he will take into the marketplace. So I'll ask this question, "Does your interaction with donors presume that the gift you seek will be their last donation to the organization? Or the first of many?"

Just to be unambiguous, let me make a recommendation regarding *Asking about Asking Again*. Interact with every prospective donor as if the project you promote is worth supporting on an ongoing basis.

> Consider a pledge as an extended 'invitation to cultivate.'
>
>  **practical tip**

> ***Prepare*** donors to continue their support.
>
> **recommendation**

Treat contributors in ways that they will appreciate in the future and that are conducive to repetition. This approach values relationships above transactions.

Our assumptions have a distinct bearing on our own behavior. And our behavior telegraphs our view of the future to those with whom we come in contact. The result is that our assumptions tend to affect the responses we receive from others.

There is a story of an aged man who lived on a craggy peak above an ancient village. Although no one knew his real name, people called him Solomon because of their high regard for his insight and wisdom. From time to time, peasants would climb the mountain to ask for his advice.

One day Billy, a mischievous young boy, decided to outsmart the wise old man. He caught a baby sparrow and plotted to conceal it in his hands and ask Solomon, "What do I hold in my hands?" When Solomon answers, "It is a bird," I will ask him, "Is the bird living or dead?" If the wise man says it is dead, I will open my hands and let the bird fly away. But if he says it is alive, I will crush it and open my hands to reveal a dead bird. In either case the old man will be wrong.

> **What *not* to say**
>
> "Your last gift was helpful, but now we need more." Instead, always be appreciative for past support. Approach future support in a way that is inspiring and motivating, but not presumptuous.
>
>  **practical tip**

So, off to the mountain Billy went, bird in hand.

Just as he had planned, Billy asked, "Solomon, I have a question for you."

"Yes, son," the old man replied.

"What is in my hand?" Billy queried.

The wise old man squinted his eyes, sniffed the air, listened intently and then announced with certainty, "It is a fragile young sparrow, son."

Billy, now certain he had tricked the sagacious man in his trap, baited him by asking, "Is the sparrow alive or dead"?

Without hesitation the savant, knowing the boy was trying to snare him, replied, "It is as you make it."

While the wise man's declaration may be too simplistic to address every gift solicitation scenario, it does offer a valuable principle for our consideration.

For example, we've all probably been approached with an unconvincing and reluctant 'request' that goes something like this: "I'm raising money to cure heart disease. You don't want to give, do you?" What kind of success would you expect from that approach?

Or similarly, "I need someone to sponsor me for the charity marathon. I'm looking for $100 sponsors, but you don't have to give that much." This approach won't secure any $100 gifts; perhaps not any support at all. Expectation comes through unmistakably in what we say and do.

Charles Kettering was an American inventor and held 140 United States patents. He was a prominent figure in the automotive industry and widely recognized for his engineering and research breakthroughs. He is quoted as saying, "High achievement always takes place in the framework of high expectation." It is remarkable how much impact our expectations have on our own achievements and on those to whom we express our expectations.

Be sure to report back to the donor on a regular basis about the progress that is being made in the campaign and the milestones that are being achieved. Give them an idea of what lies ahead.

Let's briefly revisit *The 10 Step Staircase* that was introduced in Chapter Six (see page 45). As we repeat the donor development cycle (see p.

> *High achievement always takes place in the framework of high expectation.*
>
> —Charles Kettering
> American Inventor and Industrialist

242) and begin to climb toward the 'Yes' door, we may be able to expedite our progress up the staircase. We begin the climb at a different place than we did on our first approach to a particular donor. Be prepared to abbreviate the process where appropriate, but do not ignore any of the 10 Steps.

Approach the donor with a conversation something like this, "Katie and Jason, you've been very generous over these last three years. Your $1.5 million gift to name the Betsy Armstrong Activity Room in the new Education Center has done more for Healthy Hearts than we could ever have dreamed! Your gift also brought matching gifts of $60,000 from ABC Corporation plus $300,000 from Acme, Inc. Thank you for sending your corporate dollars our direction as well. And there is no way we can tally the number of gifts we received from others who were inspired by your generosity. Thank you.

Motivate donors to continue their support.

recommendation

From the Donor's Perspective

"They used our gift as we intended. We have been informed of the progress regularly. This is a true success! We would love to continue our involvement."

viewpoint

"The building is nearly complete and we'll be moving in soon. Last December you fulfilled your pledge and we would like to ask if you would be open to a request to contribute toward the operating budget over the next year?" Or, "When would be the appropriate time for us to begin discussing your next gift?"

Notice that we have not asked for a gift, but we have introduced the idea that there will be a time to seek additional funding. It can also be helpful along the way to provide reports to keep donors informed about additional priorities and projects that lie ahead.

Ask donors to continue their support.

recommendation

To Recap

Plan of Action

◆ *Identify the donor* you want to *Ask about Asking Again.*

_____

◆ Decide *when* you should call to ask for a meeting.
___/___/___ @ ___:___

◆ *Where* is the most appropriate place to hold this meeting?

_____

◆ *Who* will join you when you meet with the prospect?

_____

◆ What materials do you need to take along when you meet?

_____

_____

_____

Evaluate your experience:

◆ What was the outcome of the call?

◆ What went well?

◆ What didn't?

◆ How do you feel about the interaction?

◆ What will you repeat in future calls?

◆ What will you avoid in future calls?

◆ What follow-up is required (next step)?

◆ Who will take the next step?

◆ When?

◆ Later, ask the donor for candid feedback/assessment.

In Closing

(or, Getting Started)

Conclusion sounds like the end of something. While this ends the book you're reading (yippee!!), my hope is that, for you, this is only the beginning of your most joyful, productive and rewarding fundraising endeavors.

So, let's get started!

I suggest that you think *big*, but start small.

What I mean is this: Cultivate a *big vision* of what you can accomplish for your charity of choice. But don't try to do it all in one day.

Start where you are. Use what you have. Do what you can.

> **Starting Over**
>
> *Nobody can go back and start a new beginning, but anyone can start today and make a new ending.*
>
> —Maria Robinson

Take small steps. Enjoy the success that comes with these modest efforts. Then push yourself to stretch just a bit further with your next endeavor.

Specifically, let me challenge you to commit to taking the following eight steps:

PLEDGE TO ACT

Step	Due date	Date Completed	Action
1.	__/__/__	__/__/__	Identify who you will cultivate first
2.	__/__/__	__/__/__	Talk to the prospect about your organization (why you're involved, etc.)
3.	__/__/__	__/__/__	Ask: "Could you ever see yourself being involved with us...?"
4.	__/__/__	__/__/__	Listen
5.	__/__/__	__/__/__	Respond accordingly
6.	__/__/__	__/__/__	Discuss what you heard with the other member of your call team
7.	__/__/__	__/__/__	Determine which step to take next
8.	__/__/__	__/__/__	Follow through as required

I commit myself to taking these steps on or before the due dates listed.

I consent to being held accountable for my actions by reporting regularly to _____ *(name).*

_____   _____

Signed   Date

To Recap

Plan of Action

- ◆ Did you accept the author's challenge to take the eight action steps listed on page 250?

- ◆ If 'Yes,' did you meet the due dates you established?

- ◆ What was *easiest* for you?

- ◆ What was most *difficult*?

- ◆ What will you repeat in the future?

- ◆ What will you *avoid* in the future?

- ◆ To whom could you recommend the Conversational Fundraising approach?

Feedback

I'm eager to hear about your experience as you apply the principles found in *Asking about Asking*. If you're willing to share your feedback and the lessons you have learned, please email us at Feedback@ AskingAboutAsking.com—we'd love to keep up with your story!

Twelve Ways You Can Help Others

If *Asking about Asking* has inspired you to transform your fundraising results, here are a dozen ways you can help others do the same:

1. Visit our web site, www.AskingAboutAsking.com for more information, book reviews, events and ideas.

2. Purchase *Asking about Asking* for each member of your favorite charity's board of trustees.

3. Write a book review for *Asking about Asking* and submit it to Barnes & Noble, Amazon.com or Borders.

4. Recommend *Asking about Asking* to a friend, colleague, professional association, civic group, alma mater, book club, or community leader.

5. Invite the author to deliver the keynote address at the annual conference of your professional society, fundraising group, corporate network or national/regional/state association.

6. Is *Asking about Asking* available in your favorite library? If not, encourage the library to add this valuable resource to their collection.

7. Post your thoughts regarding *Asking about Asking* on your blog. Your comments will help others transform their fundraising results also.

8. Ask bookstores in your area (chain or independent) to carry *Asking about Asking.*

9. Schedule a presentation on Climbing *The 10 Step Staircase* in your upcoming workshop, training session, board retreat or conference. Contact us for details.

10. Contact the book editor or philanthropy writer of your local newspaper, radio station or television network. Ask them to review *Asking about Asking* and share your story of elevating your overall fundraising efforts.

11. Assist others in purchasing the book by adding a link to www. AskingAboutAsking.com on your website.

12. Direct media inquiries regarding *Asking about Asking* to Info@ AskingAboutAsking.com or (866) 787-6626.

For more information contact:

The Institute for Conversational Fundraising™
P.O. Box 4012
Bartlesville, OK 74006

(866) 787-6626

www.AskingAboutAsking.com

Appendix A—Code of Ethical Principles and Standards

ETHICAL PRINCIPLES Adopted 1964; amended September 2007

The Association of Fundraising Professionals (AFP) exists to foster the development and growth of fundraising professionals and the profession, to promote high ethical behavior in the fundraising profession and to preserve and enhance philanthropy and volunteerism.

Members of AFP are motivated by an inner drive to improve the quality of life through the causes they serve. They serve the ideal of philanthropy, are committed to the preservation and enhancement of volunteerism; and hold stewardship of these concepts as the overriding direction of their professional life. They recognize their responsibility to ensure that needed resources are vigorously and ethically sought and that the intent of the donor is honestly fulfilled.

To these ends, AFP members, both individual and business, embrace certain values that they strive to uphold in performing their responsibilities for generating philanthropic support. AFP business members strive to promote and protect the work and mission of their client organizations.

AFP members both individual and business aspire to:

- practice their profession with integrity, honesty, truthfulness and adherence to the absolute obligation to safeguard the public trust

- act according to the highest goals and visions of their organizations, professions, clients and consciences

- put philanthropic mission above personal gain

- inspire others through their own sense of dedication and high purpose

- improve their professional knowledge and skills, so that their performance will better serve others

- demonstrate concern for the interests and well-being of individuals affected by their actions

- value the privacy, freedom of choice and interests of all those affected by their actions

- foster cultural diversity and pluralistic values and treat all people with dignity and respect

- affirm, through personal giving, a commitment to philanthropy and its role in society

- adhere to the spirit as well as the letter of all applicable laws and regulations

- advocate within their organizations adherence to all applicable laws and regulations

- avoid even the appearance of any criminal offense or professional misconduct

- bring credit to the fundraising profession by their public demeanor

- encourage colleagues to embrace and practice these ethical principles and standards

- be aware of the codes of ethics promulgated by other professional organizations that serve philanthropy

ETHICAL STANDARDS

Furthermore, while striving to act according to the above values, AFP members, both individual and business, agree to abide (and to ensure, to the best of their ability, that all members of their staff abide) by the AFP standards. Violation of the standards might subject the member to disciplinary sanctions, including expulsion, as provided in the AFP Ethics Enforcement Procedures.

Member Obligations

1. Members shall not engage in activities that harm the members' organizations, clients or profession.

2. Members shall not engage in activities that conflict with their fiduciary, ethical and legal obligations to their organizations, clients or profession.

3. Members shall effectively disclose all potential and actual conflicts of interest; such disclosure does not preclude or imply ethical impropriety.

4. Members shall not exploit any relationship with a donor, prospect, volunteer, client or employee for the benefit of the members or the members' organizations.

5. Members shall comply with all applicable local, state, provincial and federal civil and criminal laws.

6. Members recognize their individual boundaries of competence and are forthcoming and truthful about their professional experience and qualifications and will represent their achievements accurately and without exaggeration.

7. Members shall present and supply products and/or services honestly and without misrepresentation and will clearly identify the details of those products, such as availability of the products and/or services and other factors that may affect the suitability of the products and/or services for donors, clients or nonprofit organizations.

8. Members shall establish the nature and purpose of any contractual relationship at the outset and will be responsive and available to organizations and their employing organizations before, during and after any sale of materials and/or services. Members will comply with all fair and reasonable obligations created by the contract.

9. Members shall refrain from knowingly infringing the intellectual property rights of other parties at all times. Members shall address and rectify any inadvertent infringement that may occur.

10. Members shall protect the confidentiality of all privileged information relating to the provider/client relationships.

11. Members shall refrain from any activity designed to disparage competitors untruthfully.

Solicitation and Use of Philanthropic Funds

12. Members shall take care to ensure that all solicitation and communication materials are accurate and correctly reflect their organizations' mission and use of solicited funds.

13. Members shall take care to ensure that donors receive informed, accurate and ethical advice about the value and tax implications of contributions.

14. Members shall take care to ensure that contributions are used in accordance with donors' intentions.

15. Members shall take care to ensure proper stewardship of all revenue sources, including timely reports on the use and management of such funds.

16. Members shall obtain explicit consent by donors before altering the conditions of financial transactions.

Presentation of Information

17. Members shall not disclose privileged or confidential information to unauthorized parties.

18. Members shall adhere to the principle that all donor and prospect information created by, or on behalf of, an organization or a client is the property of that organization or client and shall not be transferred or utilized except on behalf of that organization or client.

19. Members shall give donors and clients the opportunity to have their names removed from lists that are sold to, rented to or exchanged with other organizations.

20. Members shall, when stating fundraising results, use accurate and consistent accounting methods that conform to the appropriate guidelines adopted by the American Institute of Certified Public Accountants (AICPA)* for the type of organization involved. (*In countries outside of the United States, comparable authority should be utilized.)

Compensation and Contracts

21. Members shall not accept compensation or enter into a contract that is based on a percentage of contributions; nor shall members accept finder's fees or contingent fees. Business members must refrain from receiving compensation from third parties derived

from products or services for a client without disclosing that third-party compensation to the client (for example, volume rebates from vendors to business members).

22. Members may accept performance-based compensation, such as bonuses, provided such bonuses are in accord with prevailing practices within the members' own organizations and are not based on a percentage of contributions.

23. Members shall neither offer nor accept payments or special considerations for the purpose of influencing the selection of products or services.

24. Members shall not pay finder's fees, commissions or percentage compensation based on contributions, and shall take care to discourage their organizations from making such payments.

25. Any member receiving funds on behalf of a donor or client must meet the legal requirements for the disbursement of those funds. Any interest or income earned on the funds should be fully disclosed.

Appendix B—Donor Bill of Rights

Philanthropy is based on voluntary action for the common good. It is a tradition of giving and sharing that is primary to the quality of life. To assure that philanthropy merits the respect and trust of the general public, and that donors and prospective donors can have full confidence in the nonprofit organizations and causes they are asked to support, we declare that all donors have these rights:

I

To be informed of the organization's mission, of the way the organization intends to use donated resources, and of its capacity to use donations effectively for their intended purposes.

II

To be informed of the identity of those serving on the organization's governing board, and to expect the board to exercise prudent judgment in its stewardship responsibilities.

III

To have access to the organization's most recent financial statements.

IV

To be assured their gifts will be used for the purposes for which they were given.

V

To receive appropriate acknowledgment and recognition.

VI

To be assured that information about their donations is handled with respect and with confidentiality to the extent provided by law.

VII

To expect that all relationships with individuals representing organizations of interest to the donor will be professional in nature.

VIII

To be informed whether those seeking donations are volunteers, employees of the organization or hired solicitors.

IX

To have the opportunity for their names to be deleted from mailing lists that an organization may intend to share.

X

To feel free to ask questions when making a donation and to receive prompt, truthful and forthright answers.

The text of this statement in its entirety was developed by the American Association of Fund-Raising Counsel (AAFRC), Association for Healthcare Philanthropy (AHP), Council for Advancement and Support of Education (CASE), and the Association of Fundraising Professionals (AFP), and adopted in November 1993.

Appendix C—Sample Gift Chart

Sample Gift Chart*

Leadership Gifts

1 gift of	$1,500,000	for a total of	$ 1,500,000
1 gift of	$1,000,000	for a total of	$ 1,000,000
3 gifts of	$ 500,000	for a total of	$ 1,500,000
6 gifts of	$ 250,000	for a total of	$ 1,500,000
11 gifts		totaling	$ 5,500,000

Major Gifts

12 gifts of	$ 100,000	for a total of	$ 1,200,000
18 gifts of	$ 50,000	for a total of	$ 900,000
36 gifts of	$ 25,000	for a total of	$ 900,000
66 gifts		totaling	$ 3,000,000

General Gifts

72 gifts of	$ 10,000	for a total of	$ 720,000
84 gifts of	$ 5,000	for a total of	$ 420,000
106 gifts of	$ 2,500	for a total of	$ 265,000
106 gifts of	<$ 2,500	for a total of	$ 95,000
368 gifts		totaling	$ 1,500,000
445 Gifts		Totaling	$10,000,000

* Notice that the Leadership and Major gifts categories constitute 17% of the donors, who contribute 85% of the dollars. Conversely, the General gifts category comprises 83% of the donors who give 15% of the dollars.

Appendix D—Types of Gifts

When seeking major contributions look beyond cash! Cash gifts often indicate a donation of income.

In a capital fundraising effort, especially seek gifts that represent a distribution of accumulation.

- ◆ Cash
- ◆ Stock or other securities (appreciated)
- ◆ Real estate—homes, farms, etc.
- ◆ Mutual funds
- ◆ Donor Advised Funds
- ◆ IRAs (avoid enormous tax liabilities)
- ◆ Trusts
- ◆ Gifts-in-kind—inventory, equipment, vehicles
- ◆ Bequests
- ◆ Insurance
- ◆ Mineral rights
- ◆ Royalties
- ◆ Intellectual property—software
- ◆ Life estates
- ◆ Charitable gift annuities
- ◆ Community foundation funds

Appendix E—Formal Gift Proposal

September 14, 20XX

Mr. and Mrs. Generous Family
1234 NW Pleasant Avenue
Anywhere, USA 54321

Re: $ 250,000 gift over three years to fund the Meals for Hungry Kids Center

Dear Libby and James,

We want to thank you for meeting with us over these last several weeks to explore your possible involvement with Making Hunger History's campaign for the new Meals for Hungry Kids Center. Your help and encouragement have been invaluable in this early stage of our fundraising effort. Thank you. And even though we have a long way to go, we are already beginning to see the 'light at the end of the tunnel.' This simply could not have happened without your involvement. Again, we say thanks.

Indeed, our leaders refuse to be content with these achievements – as impressive as they are. The board of Making Hunger History has proposed an aggressive building plan that will establish a suitable facility for this crucial work. This will enable us to more effectively serve area residents and their family members.

An architectural firm has been selected to design the new center. In addition to the building, equipment and furnishings will be secured to enhance the efficiency of the overall operation. Further, we desire to establish a fund to provide for the long term maintenance and upkeep of these facilities and the programs they will house.

We are completing the final steps of our planning process now, and want to submit this request for your consideration before the end of the year. We plan to conduct a comprehensive fundraising campaign next year and are requesting that you take a position of leadership with an early funding commitment. *Would you consider a three-year donation of $250,000 to bring hope to these needy, deserving, neglected children?* Your support will provide a strong example for many other funders to follow, propelling us to a successful conclusion to our campaign.

We will be happy to discuss the possibility of naming opportunities that may be appropriate for your gift.

If you have any questions, please feel free to call either of us. In advance, thank you for your consideration of our request.

Sincerely,

LaTisha A. Volunteer   Robert M. Cunningham
Board Chair   Executive Director

Enclosures: Case Statement
                Proposed Site Plan
                Campaign Goals Summary
                Naming Opportunities
                Campaign Cabinet
                Board of Trustees
                Other...

Appendix F—Donor/Prospect Contact Plan

Prospect name: _____

What is the *purpose* of this call?

- ☐ To share the vision for our organization.
- ☐ To cultivate a future gift.
- ☐ To secure the prospect's involvement with us (volunteer).
- ☐ To ask for a gift (Amount: $_____ -or- Range: from $_____ to $_____)
- ☐ Other: _____

_____

To be contacted by _____ and _____ (staff & volunteer)

When?   _____:_____   ____/____/____

Materials to take along: ☐ Proposal   ☐ Funding Priorities

☐ Gift range chart   ☐ Brochure(s):

☐ Other: _____

....

Was the purpose achieved? (explain)

Follow-up: **What** needs to be done?
       When?
       By **whom?**

Appendix G—Donor/Prospect Listening Guide

Careful listening equips the fundraiser with a wealth of information. This information can be strategically utilized to assist donors in achieving their philanthropic goals.

When interacting with donors and prospects, be attentive to the following topics and be prepared to explore further if the circumstances warrant.

Also be mindful that the interaction between donor and fundraiser creates a 'high trust relationship.' This confidence must constantly be safeguarded as the high value asset that it truly is.

Here are twenty topics to listen for:

1. Partialities
2. Passions
3. Pastimes
4. People
5. Philosophy
6. Pilgrimage
7. Plans
8. Policies
9. Positions (on issues)
10. Possessions
11. Prejudices
12. Preoccupations
13. Preparation
14. Pride
15. Priorities
16. Problems
17. Profession
18. Profits
19. Property
20. Pursuits

Appendix H—Donor/Prospect Contact Report

CONFIDENTIAL

Name: Contacted by:

Location (be specific):   Date ____/ ____/ ____

What I Learned Regarding:

Family (People):

Relationships:

Affinities:

Interests:

Work/Background:

Needs/Desires:

Assets / Income (Stock, Land, Rentals, Business, Possessions):

Issues/Positions:

Attitude toward personal attention/publicity:

Plans:

Glossary

Appreciation: the expression of sincere gratitude to a donor for a gift or pledge.

Association of Fundraising Professionals (AFP): a professional society (headquartered in Arlington, VA.) that fosters the development and growth of fundraising professionals, works to advance philanthropy and volunteerism and promotes high ethical standards in the fundraising profession. (Formerly the National Society of Fund Raising Executives - NSFRE.)

Ask, the: a direct request for a contribution from a specific prospective donor.

Assume: to take for granted or without proof; suppose; postulate; posit: *to assume that everyone wants peace.*

Call team: the individuals assigned to meet with a given prospective donor. The team usually consists of the CEO of the nonprofit organization and a volunteer who is a peer to the prospect.

Chief development officer (CDO): the highest-ranking development staff member responsible for a development program.

Chief executive officer (CEO): the highest-ranking executive responsible for organizational operations.

Conversational Fundraising: approaching major gift prospects in a manner that is relationship focused, mission centered, long-term oriented, permission based, inquisitive and respectful.

Cultivation: the systematic, intentional process of preparing a prospective donor to consider a gift that will advance the mission of a charitable organization.

Donor: a person who makes a voluntary contribution for a charitable purpose. By definition in this book, the finest people on earth—people who do what they don't have to do.

Donor Bill of Rights: the statement of rights provided to a donor.

Executive director: an individual who manages or directs a charitable organization's affairs. Sometimes also known as the chief executive officer (CEO).

Finest people on earth: donors and volunteers—people who do what they don't have to do.

Funder: an individual, business, foundation or other entity making monetary contributions to charitable organizations.

General gifts: contributions at the bottom of the gift chart, making up 10 to 15 percent of the total.

Gift chart: a table of information outlining the number of contributions at various giving levels needed to achieve a given fundraising goal.

Gift of convenience: a gift that is convenient for the donor to make. The gift requires little thought, and takes less effort than other giving options.

Gift of obligation: a gift for which donors sense they have no choice in making due to their own wealth, public standing, membership, etc.

Gift of significance: a contribution that is truly significant from the viewpoint of the one making the gift.

Go-away money: refers to a busy, distracted donor dismissing a fundraiser by simply writing a check.

Guessing: arriving at an opinion about something by estimate or conjecture or without having sufficient evidence to support the opinion fully.

Impulse gift: a gift made in haste. Usually occurs when the donor is emotionally moved by an introduction to the charitable cause, responds on the spot, and immediately feels like they have addressed the problem.

Leadership gifts: donations at the top of the gift chart, collectively comprising more than half of the total.

Major gifts: donations in the middle of the gift chart, making up approximately one third of the total.

Mission statement: a statement about a societal need or value that an organization proposes to address.

Nonprofit organization: an entity formed for charitable purposes and from which its trustees do not benefit financially. Sometimes called not-for-profit organization or NPO.

Not-for-profit organization: see Nonprofit organization.

NPO: see Nonprofit organization.

Peer: person who is of equal standing to another in demonstrated ability, business position, background and/or social status.

Philanthropy: love of humankind, usually expressed by an effort to enhance the well-being of humanity through personal acts of practical kindness or by financial support of a cause.

Pledge: a promise that is written, signed, and dated, to fulfill a commitment at some future time; specifically, a financial promise payable according to terms agreed to by the donor. Such pledges may be legally enforceable, subject to state law.

Principle of proportional giving: the tendency for decisions about the amount of a gift to be made in relation to some other measure, for example the total amount to be raised.

Proposal: the act of suggesting a specific contribution to be made by a particular charitable funder.

Requipping: to equip again, but differently than the original. Applying new thinking to old problems so as to generate dramatically different results.

Sincerity: being genuine, real or free of deceit, hypocrisy, or falseness; earnest. (from Dictionary.com)

Solicitation: the act of requesting a specific gift from a specific donor for a specific purpose at a specific time.

Solicitation team: see call team.

Stewardship: a process whereby an organization seeks to be worthy of continued philanthropic support, including the acknowledgment of gifts, donor recognition, the honoring of donor intent, prudent investment of gifts and the effective and efficient use of funds to further the mission of the organization.

Stewardship principle: a maxim recognizing that the work of a fundraiser is to help donors achieve their own philanthropic goals.

Strategic listening: the careful attention given to a donor prospect, especially after raising a carefully-thought-out question pertaining to the gift-making process.

Suspect: a possible source of support whose philanthropic interests appear to match those of a particular organization, but whose linkages, giving ability, and interests have not yet been confirmed.

Token gift: a contribution motivated by the desire to be included on the list of contributors, but without concern about *where* the donor's name appears on that list.

Transformational gift: a contribution large enough to truly transform the future of an organization.

Volunteer: a person who performs personal service willingly and without monetary compensation.

NOTE: Some definitions were adapted, with permission, from the Association of Fundraising Professionals (AFP) Dictionary of Fundraising Terms.

Index

Just Released!

FUNDRAI$ING
as a Career

What, Are You Crazy?

www.charitychannel.com

Just Released!

50 A$KS
in 50 Weeks

A Guide to Better Fundraising for Your Small Development Shop

www.charitychannel.com